RELIGION

AND

HUMAN RIGHTS

Religion and the Roots of Conflict

Religious Militancy or "Fundamentalism"

Universality vs. Relativism in Human Rights

Positive Resources of Religion for Human Rights

WITHDRAWN

EDITED BY JOHN KELSAY AND SUMNER B. TWISS FOR

THE PROJECT ON RELIGION AND HUMAN RIGHTS

Copyright © 1994 by The Project on Religion and Human Rights, 485 Fifth Avenue, 3rd floor, New York, NY 10017-6104; telephone/fax (212) 867-6183. All rights reserved. Printed in the United States of America.

ISBN 1-56432-141-X

Project Director: Dr. Kusumita P. Pedersen.

Co-Editors: Dr. John Kelsay, Dr. Sumner B. Twiss. **Managing Editor:** Emilie Trautmann.

Designer: Libby Bassett.

MEMBERS OF THE CONSULTATION GROUPS

The Roots of Conflict: Chair, Dr. David Little, Senior Scholar on Religion, Ethics and Human Rights, The United States Institute of Peace; Dr. John Kelsay, Department of Religion, Florida State University; Prof. John Mohawk, Department of American Studies, SUNY/Buffalo; Dr. Stanley Tambiah, Department of Anthropology, Harvard University.

Religious Militancy or "Fundamentalism": Chair, Dr. Charles Strozier, Professor of History, John Jay College of the City University of New York, Co-Director, Center on Violence and Human Survival; Dr. Leila Ahmed, Department of Women's Studies, University of Massachusetts at Amherst; Dr. John S. Hawley, Director, Southern Asia Institute, Columbia University, Chair, Department of Religion, Barnard College; Dr. Samuel Heilman, Harold M. Proshansky Professor of Jewish Studies and Sociology, Graduate Center of the City University of New York; Dr. Robert Jay Lifton, Co-Director, Center on Violence and Human Survival.

Universality vs. Relativism in Human Rights: Chair, Dr. Abdullahi An-Na'im, Executive Director, Human Rights Watch/Africa; Dr. Ann Elizabeth Mayer, Associate Professor of Law, The Wharton School, University of Pennsylvania; Dr. Sumner B. Twiss, Chair, Department of Religious Studies, Brown University; The Rev. Dr. William Wipfler, Associate on Human Rights, Office of the Anglican Observer to the United Nations (retired), formerly Director, Human Rights Office of the National Council of Churches.

Positive Resources of Religion for Human Rights: Co-Chairs, Dr. Arvind Sharma, Birks Professor of Comparative Religion, McGill University, and The Rev. Dr. Harvey Cox, Thomas Professor of Divinity, Harvard Divinity School; Dr. Margaret Guider, O.F.M., Weston School of Theology; The Hon. Talat Sait Halman, Chair, Near Eastern Languages and Literatures, New York University, Representative to UNESCO, former Minister of Culture, Turkey; Dr. Susannah Heschel, Abba Hillel Silver Professor of Jewish Studies, Case Western Reserve University; The Rev. Dr. Robert Traer, Secretary General, International Association on Religious Freedom; The Rev. Dr. Preston Williams, Houghton Professor of Theology and Contemporary Change, Harvard Divinity School.

HONORARY CHAIRS

The Most Reverend Desmond Tutu, Archbishop of Capetown and Metropolitan of the Church of the Province of South Africa, and The Hon. Cyrus Vance, former United States Secretary of State.

STEERING COMMITTEE

Co-Chairs: The Right Reverend Paul Moore, Jr., Episcopal Bishop of New York (retired), and Rabbi J. Rolando Matalon, Congregation B'nai Jeshurun.

Members of the Steering Committee: Dr. Abdullahi An-Na'im, Executive Director, Human Rights Watch/Africa; The Reverend Stephen Chinlund, Director, Episcopal Social Services; Dr. Diana Eck, Professor of Comparative Religion and Indian Studies, Harvard University; Osborn Elliott, Chair, Citizens Committee for New York City; Frederick Herter, M.D., President Emeritus, The American University of Beirut; Gara LaMarche, Executive Director, Human Rights Watch/Free Expression Project; Mrs. Margaret Lang; The Reverend Patricia A. Reeberg; The Right Reverend Sir Paul Reeves, Dean, Te Rau Kahikatea Theological College; John Phillip Santos, Executive Producer, Channel Thirteen/WNET; Dr. Charles Strozier, Professor of History, John Jay College/CUNY; The Most Reverend Joseph Sullivan, Episcopal Vicar for Human Services, Catholic Diocese of Brooklyn; The Rev. Dr. William L. Wipfler, Associate for Human Rights, Office of the Anglican Observer to the United Nations (retired).

BOARD OF ADVISORS

Robert Bernstein, Chair, Human Rights Watch; The Rev. Dr. Harvey Cox, Thomas Professor of Divinity, Harvard Divinity School; Walter Cronkite, Journalist; The Rev. Miguel d'Escoto, Fundación Nicaraguese pro Desarollo Communitario Integral, former Foreign Minister, Nicaragua; Marian Wright Edelman, President, Children's Defense Fund; Hamilton Fish, Human Rights Watch; Congressman Tony Hall, U.S. House of Representatives; The Hon. Talat Sait Halman, Chairman, Near Eastern Languages and Literatures, New York University, former Minister of Culture, Turkey; Prof. Oren R. Lyons, Director, Native American Studies, State University of New York at Buffalo; Dr. Martin E. Marty, Director, The Fundamentalism Project, Fairfax M. Cone Distinguished Service Professor of the History of Modern Christianity, University of Chicago; James Merrill, Poet; Jessye Norman, Singer; John Oakes, The New York Times; Senator Claiborne Pell, U.S. Senate; James Taylor, Musician.

Organizations for purposes of identification only.

Dedication

Dedicated to the blessed memory of
Rabbi Marshall T. Meyer
Founding Co-Chair of the Project on Religion and Human Rights
who consecrated his life to the struggle for human rights.

Contents

Terms: "Human Rights" and "Religion"

HUMAN RIGHTS

For the purposes of this book, "human rights" are understood as the set of rights articulated in the thirty articles of the Universal Declaration of Human Rights, a statement of principles proclaimed by the United Nations in 1948, and in related international treaties. These treaties include the two international human rights Covenants, which the United Nations adopted in 1966 and which give legal form to the Universal Declaration. Nations that ratify the Covenants and other human rights treaties are legally bound to maintain treaty provisions. It is the responsibility of the international community to hold governments accountable to their treaty obligations.

The fifty-three articles of the Covenant on Civil and Political Rights guarantee rights such as freedom of thought and expression, freedom from arbitrary arrest and torture, and freedoms of movement and peaceful assembly. The thirty-one articles of the Covenant on Economic, Social and Cultural Rights provide for rights such as the right to work and receive fair wages, to the protection of the family, to adequate standards of living, to education, and to health care.

Together, the Universal Declaration and the international Covenants with the Optional Protocols are known as "The International Bill of Rights." Numerous subsequent treaties elaborate aspects of this Bill of Rights, including conventions on:

• Prevention and Punishment of Genocide (adopted in 1948)
• Elimination of Racial Discrimination (1965)

- Elimination of Discrimination against Women (1979)
- The Status of Refugees (1951) and Protocol on Refugees (1966)
- Rights of the Child (1989)
- Elimination of Discrimination Based on Religion or Belief (1981)
- Draft Declaration on the Rights of Indigenous Peoples, as agreed upon by members of the United Nations Working Group in 1993; the next step in the process toward U.N. adoption will be submission to the U.N. Commission on Human Rights.

International debate continues on which rights are to be accepted as universally normative and on the means of translating such acceptance into legal guarantees of human rights.

The text of the International Bill of Human Rights is available from the United Nations Department of Public Information: (212) 963-1234. Texts of the Bill of Human Rights and other seminal human rights treaties are available in *Twenty-Five Human Rights Documents*, J. Paul Martin, ed., (New York: Columbia University Press, 1994).

RELIGION

For the purposes of this book, "religion" is understood as a world view or set of beliefs, along with a value system and way of life embodying and expressing these beliefs. A "religion" typically derives its values and practices from some authority, whether personal or non-personal, beyond, underlying, or deeply implicit in ordinary reality. Religious traditions provide their adherents with a comprehensive understanding of the world and identify the place and role of human beings and other sentient beings within that world. Religions also attempt to provide answers to the most basic questions of existence: the origin and meaning of existence; the nature of life and death; the meaning of suffering and ways to overcome it; the nature of evil and ways to overcome it; and the ultimate destiny of human life and of all life.

A "religion" calls on its adherents to live according to its values through a prescribed set of practices and relationships that may affect many aspects of personal and social life. Not merely a matter of belief or doctrine, a "religion" constitutes an integral culture, which can form personal and social identity and can influence experience and behavior in concrete and significant ways.

Co-Chairs' Introduction

The Project on Religion and Human Rights has been undertaken in the conviction that the complex relation between religion and human rights is not adequately understood and that the need for a new inquiry is critical at this time, when this relation is changing rapidly and affecting the lives of millions. The studies in this volume were carried out in the Project's first year. This has been the effort of many collaborators with diverse expertise, as well as different cultural and religious backgrounds. All of us, however, believe in the urgency of the issues that we raise here. This is the first step in a process which we hope will lead not only to clearer understanding, but also to increased cooperation and practical action.

Throughout the world there are many violent conflicts in which religion is a factor. Massive human rights abuses, war, atrocities, and genocide continue. At the same time, movements for freedom and reform have brought new life to millions. These, too, often have a religious dimension. The map of the world has changed radically, and so has the pattern of events. There is a sense that what is happening in the world is a seismic shift in the dynamics of war, the direction of history, and perhaps in the very destiny of humanity. Similar world-transforming events have taken place before: for example, the fall of Rome, the spread of Buddhism and Islam, the arrival of Europeans in the Americas, the Industrial Revolution, and the two World Wars. The difference, however, between those historical moments and today has to do with the rapidity and the seemingly chaotic quality of events. Steep waves of violence, caused by invisible currents and winds of change, erupt in far-flung places for seemingly different reasons. Underneath, deeper tides are in motion—the currents of the human soul itself. To grapple with the world crisis, we must attempt to fathom the mysterious workings of the human spirit, which sometimes fill the world with grace and sometimes with demonic cruelty.

If we think of religion not only as a total world view of persons and communities, but also as a set of sometimes frenzied emotions which well up within individuals and groups, we see that a grasp of the religious dimension of world conflict is essential. Clearly, many causes come together to create a Bosnia, a Northern Ireland, a Punjab, or a Lebanon: for example, ethnic conflicts, economic inequities, historic land disputes. But when religion becomes a channel for these forces, and becomes a symbol under which they clash, a new and peculiar dynamic is added. When nationalism and religion mix, violence can occur which carries all before it.

Why does religious belief produce both peacemakers and hate-mongers? What is the nature of the tension, sometimes fruitful, sometimes destructive, between universal human rights and the particular value systems of religious traditions? Is democratic liberalism itself a kind of fundamentalism? Have economic and cultural imperialism somehow caused as a backlash developments we now deplore? How can secular human rights experts, religious leaders of all faiths, and persons of opposing political convictions and different social values work together more closely? These are some of the questions that have animated our inquiry in the past year.

We have asked, Who has the right to speak about rights? And we have acknowledged that in any society the most marginalized groups must be heard. We must listen with special attention to the voices of those who have lived through conflict and oppression and who have been themselves the victims of human rights abuses. We have tried to bring into the process of study not only the analysis of specialists, but also testimony from the field, as well as the views of participants from different areas of endeavor, and different religions and cultures. We have been challenged by our own participants to give a fuller account of the experiences and the proposals of women and indigenous peoples.

We are keenly aware of the need to be self-critical in our traditions, in our communities, and in our individual lives. This applies not only to our religions and our personal values, but also to the assumptions of our approaches to academic study and of public policy. In our investigation we must be prepared to seek far-reaching, radical, and arduous solutions and to accept the challenge of implementing them. Although we do not suppose dialogue will soon produce a single accepted interpretation of any religious tradition—or of human rights— we are committed to the critical process of dialogue, re-examination, and exploration.

We dedicate this work to Rabbi Marshall Meyer, who was a founding co-chair of this Project but did not live to see its manifestation. Marshall embraced the fight for human rights with every fiber of his being, and his struggle issued from the very root of his religious commitment. As a person of profound faith, as a firm believer in the image of the divine in every human being, he could not but embrace the preservation of the sanctity of life and the dignity of life with boldness, passion, and immense vigor and courage.

To Marshall, being religious meant being a witness to this sanctity and dignity, responding over and over again with a resounding "Yes" to the question, "Am I my brother's and my sister's keeper?" Time and again he conquered fear with courage, and whether in the Argentine jails or in the streets of Buenos Aires, at the time of the Nazi fascist military junta, whether in New York City, embracing the cause of homeless people, or people with AIDS, or in Northern Ireland, or in the Middle East as an ardent lover of Zion, Marshall exemplified the values to which this book is dedicated.

Marshall loved stories. One of his favorite stories, which he told again and again, was this: A person was lost in a dense, dark forest. As the daylight faded into the lengthening shadows of dusk and the thickness of night gathered, the person became more and more afraid. For three days and nights, he felt painfully and hopelessly lost. He became desperate.

On the fourth day he saw a monster approaching him from afar. He filled his pockets with rocks and prepared a heavy club with which to defend himself. His heart beat wildly in his breast. Perspiration gathered on his brow, and the monster loomed larger and larger. It was as tall as a human being. He crouched behind some bushes, grabbing some of the sharpened stones as he prepared to attack.

Frozen in fear, he slowly realized that the monster was a human being. He threw the stones away, but kept the club, just in case. When the person was all but upon him, he threw the club away and embraced the person. It was his own sister, who had come to look for him.

With this story Marshall exemplified the encounter that is necessary between human beings. We are not monsters to each other; we are brothers and sisters.

It is high time that the religious dimension of the human rights struggle be examined in concert by persons of many faiths, nationalities, and disciplines. The Project on Religion and Human Rights does not pretend to represent the world or to engage all the many issues that might concern us. But we aspire to create a momentum by which the religious dynamic of conflicts will be understood more clearly, the reasons why religion can be a beneficent or malign force for human rights be better known, and ways to begin dealing with this power be identified. We seek also to mobilize for peace and justice the positive forces in the world's spiritual traditions and in their core teachings on compassion, human dignity, and the value of life.

Our special thanks go to Dr. Kusumita P. Pedersen, who almost single-handedly created and guided the Project. And to all the others who helped in so many ways, we extend our deepest gratitude.

This publication has been made possible by a grant for this purpose from the Ford Foundation. We acknowledge the Foundation's assistance with special thanks. We also wish to thank the Rockefeller Foundation, Henry Luce III, the Rockefeller Brothers Fund, the John Merck Fund, and the Edward S. Moore Foundation for their support for the establishment of the Project.

The Right Reverend Paul Moore, Jr.
Rabbi J. Rolando Matalon
Co-Chairs

Note from the Editors

This collection of papers attempts to move beyond earlier discussions of religion and human rights. Most previous efforts have focused largely on the question of the general compatibility of human rights with the fundamental premises of discrete religious traditions construed in their normative or ideal formulations. In contrast with these efforts, the present essays attempt to address in a systematic way some of the hard, practical, and critical issues and tensions faced by human rights advocates when dealing with religions in the international arena as well as in particular social and cultural contexts. In thus raising systematic questions about religion and the roots of conflict, fundamentalism and religious militancy, the intersection between cultural particularity and the international human rights regime, and the constructive resources of religious traditions for human rights advocacy, this volume has been guided by a more praxis-oriented collaboration between scholars and professional human rights advocates. It is our belief that this collaboration has brought our studies closer to the nerve of real-world concerns about religion and human rights, and that this sort of collaboration offers a cogent paradigm for future inquiry on this subject.

We want to take this opportunity to thank not only the Consultation Groups of the Project for their intensive labors, but also those behind the scenes, most particularly Kusumita Pedersen, Executive Director of the Project, Managing Editor Emilie Trautmann, and Designer Libby Bassett. We also wish to express our appreciation to the Co-Chairs of the Consultation Groups, who, in selecting us to act as the Co-Editors for this volume, provided us with a valuable opportunity to become even more deeply engaged in the issues and collaborative work of the Project. The task has been challenging and deeply rewarding, not least for being associated with human rights advocates and scholars of religion deeply concerned about the future of human affairs and the well-being of the world's peoples.

John Kelsay
Sumner B. Twiss

This paper is the result of an extensive collaborative endeavor, in particular by members of the Consultation Group on Religion and the Roots of Conflict, brought together by the Project on Religion and Human Rights. Members of the Consultation Group include John Kelsay, David Little, John Mohawk, and Stanley Tambiah. The process of writing this paper began when a preliminary outline of assumptions, probable religious sources of enmity, and conditions of conflict was drafted by David Little. The group solicited responses from persons with expertise in a number of particular cases of religious conflict. Of these, a number submitted written responses. Members of the Consultation Group then met to hear responses from three others: Professor Vigen Guroian of Loyola University, Baltimore; David Steele of the Center for Strategic and International Studies at Georgetown University; and Professor George Majeska of American University. Subsequent discussion by members of the Consultation Group, with participation by Project Director Kusumita Pedersen, indicated the importance of a number of extensions and additions to the earlier outline, which were incorporated into a working paper drafted by John Kelsay. Comments by participants from other Consultation Groups of the Project on Religion and Human Rights, especially S. B. Twiss, have been incorporated by Kelsay into this final version of the paper. This is the place to express gratitude to all those who contributed their opinions and expertise.

It should be noted that the findings of another project in which Kelsay, Little, and Tambiah are participants, the U.S. Institute of Peace working group on Religion, Nationalism, and Religious Intolerance, inform this paper. Those wishing to consult these findings may examine the various "country reports" authored by David Little. A number are forthcoming; those published thus far include *Sri Lanka: The Invention of Enmity* (Washington, D.C.: USIP Press, 1994). Also relevant is *Ukraine: The Legacy of Intolerance* (Washington, D.C.: USIP Press, 1992).

1

Religion and the Roots of Conflict

Just a few days prior to the killing of more than two dozen Palestinians during Friday prayers in Hebron, a *New York Times* article focused on militant sentiment among Jewish settlers in the West Bank.[1] With almost uncanny prescience, Joel Greenberg's article recorded some of the attitudes that formed the background for Baruch Goldstein's actions. "The time has come for a decision about what kind of state we [Israelis] want here," said Binyamin Kahane (son of the late rabbi). "The people have to decide whether they want a Jewish state, which means annexing the territories, evicting the Arabs, having Jewish and Zionist education instead of Western education, and putting the media in national Zionist hands. There's a fundamental contradiction between a Jewish state and a democratic state." Other members of the small but determined group of settlers that make up the core membership of the Kach and Kahane Chai parties spoke of their struggle against enemies both internal and external. With respect to the former, said one, settlers are engaged in a war for the soul of Israel, much the same as the Maccabean struggle with Hellenism during the second century B.C.E. As to external enemies, Lenny Goldberg, another member of the group, left no doubt about the seriousness of the settlers: "We're in a war, and in a war there are no innocent people.... [Palestinians are all] guilty by association."

The timing of Greenberg's article, and the special interest of the United States in Arab-Israeli relations, make the story of the settlers particularly urgent. But attitudes of settlers quoted in the article are hardly strange. Indeed, the connections between religion and conflict appear as such an integral part of the current world scene that one might be forgiven for the judgment "That is

---

[1] Joel Greenberg, "Settlement Vows Fight on Peace Plan," *New York Times,* February 21, 1994, p. A4.

yesterday's news." In former Yugoslavia, Armenia and Azerbaijan, India, Sri Lanka, Egypt, and Sudan, news of violence in which religion is presumed to be a factor is by now familiar.

It must be said, however, that newspaper reports, even those as informative as Greenberg's, often raise as many questions as they answer. For those wishing to understand the role of religion in contemporary conflicts, the following questions deserve particular attention.

(1) Insofar as one can speak of religion as a root cause of contemporary conflicts, are there patterns to be identified in the various cases? For example, are there commonalities, as well as distinctions, between the role of Islam in the Sudanese conflict and the role of Buddhism in Sri Lanka's civil war? To put it another way: Is it useful to speak of *religion* as a root of conflict? Or should one only speak about specific religious traditions in particular instances of violence?

(2) In contemporary conflicts, what is the relation of religion to factors such as ethnicity and race? One sometimes hears, for example, that the conflict in former Yugoslavia has little to do with religion and that the parties are divided by ethno-national identity. At the same time, others urge that religion is the crucial factor and that ethnicity is a function of religious identity.

(3) Even as discussions of ethnicity or race complicate discussions of the role of religion in conflicts, so do arguments appealing to such non-religious factors as economic, demographic, or political conditions. What shall one say, for example, to commentators who argue that conflicts in Sri Lanka have little to do with Buddhism and have everything to do with the failure of national programs for economic development and job creation? In cases of conflict, does religion "stand on its own feet" as a root of violence, or is it simply a function of economic distress or overpopulation?

(4) What is the relation between past and present in the phenomenon of religious violence? Should we think of contemporary conflicts as something new—as a kind of radical departure from such pre-20th-century examples as the crusades, conquests of indigenous peoples by colonizing powers, or anti-Jewish pogroms? Or do contemporary and historic cases of religious conflicts have something in common?

Each of these questions (and no doubt others) deserves considerable attention. We cannot hope to answer them in this short paper. We do, however, address them, and thereby hope to advance discussion of the role(s) religion plays—as an aspect of the problem and also of the solution—in contemporary conflicts.

PATTERNS IN RELIGIOUS VIOLENCE

Religion appeals to many human needs. Part of the special genius of religion, however, lies in its ability to provide persons and groups with a sense of identity, what we might call a "place in the universe." Through the repetition of stories, symbols, rituals, credal pronouncements, scriptural texts, and other practices, religious traditions encourage the development of ways of thinking, feeling, and acting that serve to order the lives of persons and groups around some notion(s) of a reality that is considered sacred.[1] Described in this way, such a reality serves to orient persons and groups in terms of the performance of a mission and/or the maintenance of a set of values that is taken to be right, good, or true in the sense that it is proper for human beings to live by it. As often noted, notions of sacred reality tend to be expressed in ways that suggest their importance for resolving such great existential questions as the origins of life and death or the meaning of suffering. In connection with religious violence, it is perhaps more significant to note the ways that notions of sacred reality, and the practices in which they are embedded, encourage a sense of identification that we might call "group feeling."

With these factors in mind, an examination of contemporary cases of religious violence indicates the following as patterns that appear with reasonable consistency.

(1) The division of human communities into an "in" group and an "out" group: In the course of fostering group feeling, religion serves to motivate behaviors important to personal and social integration. Cooperation, sharing, and altruism can all be related to the sense of identity that religious traditions provide. At the same time, group feeling can be supportive of behaviors that differentiate human beings by drawing lines between groups. Distinctions between those who are "in" and those who are "out" are simply part of the differentiating role of religion in human consciousness. In situations of conflict, these distinctions are heightened, sometimes to the extent that one may speak of groups "demonizing" one another. Thus Serbs speak of the fact that Muslims or Croats cannot be trusted and tell stories of unspeakable atrocities performed by these "out" groups. Similar patterns exist when Croats speak of Serbs and increasingly (although with more obvious and recent cases in mind), when Muslims speak of

---

[1] With slight variations, the characterization of religion here is taken from David Little and Sumner B. Twiss, *Comparative Religious Ethics: A New Method,* (San Francisco: Harper & Row, 1978); see especially chapter 3.

Serbs or Croats.[1] One should further note that divisions *between* groups do not capture the full extent of the "in" and "out" group distinction. In a number of cases (perhaps most), members of the "in" group make further differentiations between those who are *truly* "in" and those who are not. The latter designation includes traitors, apostates, backsliders, or others whose behavior suggests that they do not participate fully in the feeling that unifies the group. In examining the history of religions, many commentators argue that such divisions of the world pertain particularly to those traditions that are monotheistic and claim rights to a more or less exclusive revelation. It should be said that in contemporary conflicts, this generalization does not hold. Sinhalese Buddhists behave according to an "in" group/"out" group division, as do their Tamil opponents. Militant Hindus draw lines between Hindus and Muslims, just as Muslims draw lines between themselves and Christians or practitioners of indigenous traditions in Sudan. Indeed, it is likely that over time no tradition really escapes the tendency to divide the world of human communities. Even traditions with inclusivist strategies for dealing with otherness usually carry out these strategies by encompassing or incorporating other people into a hierarchy consistent with their own framework. Rarely does one find groups behaving, in the face of difference, according to the seemingly simple standard of respect for others. This standard is, we note, at the heart of most conceptions of human rights and of such internationally-recognized human rights instruments as the Universal Declaration of Human Rights and the Declaration on the Elimination of All Forms of Intolerance and of Discrimination Based on Religion or Belief.

(2) The development of narratives that legitimate the "in" group in a struggle with the "out" group: Continuing our emphasis on the role of religion in developing personal and group identity, we note that telling stories, performing rituals, reciting creeds, and practicing other forms of religious expression can all serve this purpose. In some cases, the relationship between religion and group life is further expressed in architecture, cuisine, music, and styles of dress. All can serve to reinforce differentiations among various groups.

One very powerful mode of expression, especially important in a number of contemporary conflicts, takes a narrative form. Group feeling is directed, shaped, and sustained through narratives that explain its history, especially in relation to others. One uses "history" carefully in this context; while such narratives have an historical form and usually reflect some aspect of historical reality, they are not historical in the strict or academic sense. In a number of cases, they are fairly

---

[1] See the material collected on (in particular) Serbian practices of rape, treatment of prisoners of war, and the pursuit of the policy of ethnic cleansing in Roy Gutman, *Witness to Genocide* (New York: Macmillan, 1993).

recent inventions intended to serve the purposes of national or state development through fostering group feeling.

Thus a number of analysts claim that the contemporary narrative establishing the necessity of a Sinhala Buddhist nation in Sri Lanka was developed in the late 19th century and thereafter. Its most immediate connection was with reactions against European colonial rule and Christian missionary activity. While the narrative builds on material from scriptural and especially chronicle sources, its current form is thus of recent origin. Similar claims are made in the case of Serbian and Croat historical memory; even the northern Sudanese notion of a civilizing mission on the frontiers of Islam is linked most directly to the Mahdist struggles of the latter 19th century. We cannot sort out all the scholarly issues connected with these narratives. The claim that, strictly speaking, they are not historical, like the claim that they are of recent origin, serves mainly to remind those wishing to understand contemporary religious violence that current, especially militant, conceptions are not the whole story of any religious tradition. Further, such claims suggest that Sinhalese Buddhists or Serbs or northern Sudanese may be able to foster other, less combative versions of a group history. We shall return to this point.

In their current forms, the narratives of Sinhalese Buddhists or Serbian Christians or Muslims in northern Sudan do play a crucial role in religious violence, however. In effect, these narratives legitimate the "in" group in a struggle with "out" groups. Especially for those whose history includes an experience of foreign rule or oppression, religio-historical narratives serve (or served) the purpose of preserving group identity during hard times. At the same time, such narratives currently serve to incriminate or demonize various "out" groups, suggesting the necessity of efforts to obtain revenge for past wrongs or to defend sacred values by limiting the powers of the "out" group.

(3) This analysis leads to perhaps the most important pattern in contemporary religious violence: the legitimation of the use of armed force in struggles with an "out" group. Such legitimation can involve a number of features, including (i) formal appeals to a moral tradition indicating the conditions under which military action is justified; (ii) promotion of narratives [see (2) above] indicating the criminality of an "out" group or the threat it poses to "in" group values (or even "in" group existence); and (iii) reference to a mission in which military action, at least under certain conditions, is legitimate. The discourse of groups at this point is quite complex and usually involves a combination of these and other features.

(4) Finally, the justification for resorting to armed force is usually connected with an "in" group need to *dominate within a given territory*. The territory in question can be strictly delimited, as in the Sinhalese notion of Sri Lanka as a Buddhist land or the Serbian notion of Greater Serbia. In other cases it may in-

volve, at least as a theoretical claim, the entire world, as in the case of Islam and some forms of Christianity. It must be said, of course, that domination as envisioned by "in" groups does not necessarily entail resort to armed force. In many cases domination as a goal can be accomplished by popular movements, missions, ordinary politics, or other more or less peaceful activities. Nevertheless, if the goal of domination is considered important enough to the expression or defense of sacred values, force is maintained at least as an option of last resort.

RELIGION AND IDENTITY

The relationships between religion and ethnicity, race, and other terms by which groups of people may be classified are extremely complex. In former Yugoslavia, for example, the identity of Serbs is tied to linguistic factors. Rather quickly one notes that the spoken language of Serbs is very close to that of Croats, however; thus most linguists approach Serbo-Croatian as a single entity, suggesting that spoken language in and of itself is not the phenomenon that constitutes the identity of Serbs.

Written language constitutes another issue. As has often been noted, Serbian is written in Cyrillic, Croatian in Latin characters. Careful scrutiny of this difference still indicates the limits of a narrow focus on language as an identifying feature of warring groups in former Yugoslavia, however. The vast majority of Serbs and Croats identify with religious traditions tied to the choice of alphabet. The use of Cyrillic characters is embedded in the worship practices of Orthodox Christianity, while Latin characters point to historic ties between Croatians and the Roman Catholic Church. Further explorations into Serbian identity involve connections between Orthodox Christianity, group feeling, and claims to a particular territory; again, as often noted, the province of Kosovo occupies a special place in Serbian memory. Thus, one may speak of the classification "Serb" as involving territorial claims, as well as religious and linguistic factors.

The conclusion one draws from the conflict in former Yugoslavia and a number of other contemporary conflicts is that it is difficult to separate religion from other factors in describing group identity. Indeed, the preference of some analysts for terms such as "ethnic identity" in describing the factors contributing to conflicts appears to miss the fact that, for many peoples, *religion is intrinsically a part of the sense of ethnicity.* As some would put it, "One who is not Orthodox cannot be Serbian." Or, in another case, "All Armenians are Orthodox, even those who are not baptized."[1] In these cases, a particular religious tradition is so bound to group identity that those who speak the language or are offspring of those speaking the language are, almost by definition, a part of the tradition.

By comparison with the Yugoslavian case, religious identities in Sudan seem to be more distinct from ethnicity. In such cases the religious factor does not appear as less important, however; indeed, it could be argued that in many cases religion functions to provide a collective identity that makes other loyalties objects of suspicion. Thus, much of the conflict in Sudan may be analyzed in terms of the tension between the collective identity provided by Islam to parts of the population (particularly in the North) and by the tribal loyalties characteristic of many in the South and West. From one perspective the efforts to Islamize public life in Sudan, and the resistance of various factions to these efforts, are simply one part of a long effort by members of a community called to struggle against all partial loyalties that stand in the way of the universal justice of God. Whether their appropriations of the tradition are justified or not, it seems clear that the term "Muslim" and the practices associated with it provide many northern Sudanese with their primary identity. That the same people also sometimes refer to themselves as "Arabs" does not indicate an identity separate from Islam; the reference is intended to strengthen the connections between northern Sudanese and groups historically identified with Islam, thereby further dissociating Muslims in Sudan from indigenous African or tribal forms of identity.

We cannot resolve questions pertaining to the relationships among religion, ethnicity, race, and other indicators of identity for every current case of conflict.[2] *That there is ample evidence of a religious factor in the identity of many groups of people, however, seems beyond dispute.*

---

[1] These quotations are cited on the basis of testimony by experts (see opening acknowledgments) who indicate they are oft-repeated by Serbian and Armenian activists and religious leaders.

[2] In light of the evidence that Serbs in particular have employed rape as a tool in the campaign to "purify" sections of Bosnia from the "taint" of Muslim and Croat presence, one might consider the role of gender in the differentiation that we have been stressing between "in" and "out" groups. As Catherine McKinnon and others emphasize, rape attacks women as women; further, rape must be interpreted as part of a continuum of behaviors by which men subordinate and express their "will to power" in relation to women. See McKinnon, "Turning Rape into Pornography: Postmodern Genocide" and "Rape, Genocide, and Women's Human Rights," as well as essays by other authors collected in *Mass Rape: The War against Women in Bosnia-Herzegovina,* ed. Alexandra Stiglmayer (Lincoln: University of Nebraska, 1994).

At the same time, most interpreters note that the Muslim women of Bosnia are also targeted because they are Muslims; the analysis of rape as a tool or weapon in the policy of ethnic cleansing suggests as much. Here again, without denying the importance of gender as a distinctive notion that contributes to conflict in the former Yugoslavia, one sees the role of religion in conflict. One need not--in this case, ought not--ignore the intersection between religion and gender. Of analyses that do ignore this intersection,

RELIGIOUS AND NON-RELIGIOUS FACTORS IN CONFLICTS

Questions pertaining to the relationship of religious and economic, demographic, and/or political factors in human behavior are at least as old as Marx's writings. As with terms used to indicate identity, these questions are very complex. In this paper they are raised by those who argue that contemporary conflicts are really about economic interests, or are a function of overpopulation or of political competition. The argument can be made in several ways. In former Yugoslavia, for example, one notes the competition for power engendered by the death of Marshal Tito and the end of the Cold War; in this context, political figures such as Slobodan Milosevic and Franjo Tudjman have found it useful to appeal to religious symbols in competing for power. From the standpoint of certain sectors in the Serbian or Croatian populations, such appeals are all the more powerful because of economic distress; high inflation and unemployment create a sense of desperation to which the group feeling referred to above is one response. The conclusion of such an analysis is that religion is not so much a root of conflict as a tool used by those seeking power and security.

Similar arguments are made in the case of Sri Lanka.[1] Here, the failure of programs of economic development creates a sense of scarcity, a sense for which group feeling is again adopted or created as a response. For many analyzing the conflict between Sinhalese and Tamils, such arguments have a special appeal, since official Buddhist texts present a universalistic message, the meaning of which must be stretched (to say the least) in order to justify the type of group feelings associated with contemporary Sinhalese nationalism.

In the Sri Lankan case, such arguments appear to be motivated by at least two considerations. First, some analysts suppose that we should distinguish a particular set of scriptures, ritual practices, beliefs, or other items associated with a classical or true or foundational expression of Theravada Buddhism, on one hand, from the use of Buddhist sources in subsequent historical periods, on the other. Second, and closely related, some suppose it important to maintain some distinction between Theravada Buddhism and Sinhalese nationalism as a way of accounting for the fact that some representatives of the former tradition dissent from the fusion of their tradition with Sinhalese group feeling. We are certainly

---

McKinnon's observation will serve: "The result is that these rapes are grasped in either their ethnic or religious particularity, as attacks on a culture, meaning men, or in their sex specificity, meaning as attacks on women. But not as both at once...." In this case one sees "rape as genocide, rape directed toward women because they are Muslim or Croatian." ("Rape, Genocide, and Women's Human Rights," p. 188).

[1] In particular, these issues were raised by University of Virginia Professor of Anthropology H.L. Seniveratne in a written response to David Little's outline (see opening acknowledgments).

sympathetic with these claims, as well as with the larger point concerning the interactions between religion and economic (or demographic or political) factors in contemporary conflicts. Indeed, the need to account for religious dissent within groups is present not only in discussing the role of religion in Sri Lanka, but also in every case of religious conflict of which we are aware.[1] Unless, however, we are willing to accept the thesis that Sinhalese nationalists' appeals to Buddhism are an expression of bad faith, or are really a disguised expression of economic or political interests, it seems we must accept that religion is a part of the picture of intercommunal strife in Sri Lanka. Religion is thus *a* root of conflict, interacting with economic and other factors to bring about violence among various groups of people.[2]

RELIGION IN PAST AND PRESENT CONFLICTS

The notion that religion interacts with economic and other factors, and thus is one of several roots of conflict, leads us to discuss some historical dimensions of religious violence. We have been arguing that it is part of the genius of religious traditions to provide persons and groups with a sense of identity, a place in the universe. This sense, which we have called group feeling, seems to address a

---

[1] The point made here with respect to the phenomenon of intra-communal dissent may be illustrated, for example, by the fact that important representatives of Serbian Orthodoxy are known to dissent from the policies of Slobodan Milosevic or of the Bosnian Serbs, or that representatives of Islam criticize the behavior of the regime in Khartoum. Further, the distinction between the "true" expression of a particular tradition and subsequent interpretations or uses of it should be acknowledged as an important one, particularly as one tries to understand the ways representatives of Buddhism (or Christianity or Islam) formulate their criticisms of the behavior of members of particular groups.

At the same time, the distinction between "true" and "false" expressions of faith is not one that is simple to make. When analysts make a commitment to the scriptural or classical forms of a religious tradition, they deny the obvious fact that religious traditions change over time. To stay with the Sri Lankan case, it is certainly true that the Pali canon presents a critically important formulation of Theravada Buddhist practices. Whether we, as analysts, should judge that formulation superior to the "chronicles literature" that Sinhalese nationalists fuse with Pali scripture, is, however, not particularly germane to the task at hand. Insofar as "religion" and "religious" are terms by which we classify the behavior of Sinhalese nationalists and others, they do not express judgments about the validity of particular interpretations of a tradition, but about the intentions or motivations of groups of people.

[2] For purposes of identifying the lineage of this approach, it is useful to mention Max Weber's notion of religion as a factor having "relative independence" in motivating behavior. Max Weber, "The Social Psychology of the World Religions," in H.H. Gerth and C. Wright Mills, eds. and trans., *From Max Weber: Essays in Sociology* (New York: Oxford University Press, 1946), pp. 267-301.

crucial aspect of human psychology in that it serves the double purpose of integrating members of an "in" group and of differentiating them from members of an "out" group. In this connection, one may understand violence as one way that groups of people seek to establish boundaries between themselves and others, boundaries intended to protect a communal way of life, to advance the cause of truth or justice, or in general to secure a place in the universe. With this understanding in mind, one is justified in thinking that the potential for religion to be a root of conflict is always present in human societies. Certainly, there is ample evidence for such a judgment in the multitude of crusades, pogroms, and other events associated with the history of religious traditions. The differentiating role of religion plays its part in the history referred to in the Declaration on the Elimination of All Forms of Intolerance and of Discrimination Based on Religion or Belief:

> The disregard and infringement of human rights and fundamental freedoms, in particular of the right to freedom of thought, conscience, religion, or whatever belief, have brought, directly or indirectly, wars and great suffering to mankind. [Preamble, para. 3]

From one perspective, then, one must see contemporary religious violence as an expression of tendencies always present in the religious life of humanity and which have made themselves felt in a variety of historical contexts. At the same time, the specific ways in which religion contributes to group feeling are historically quite diverse, as are the economic and other factors with which religion interacts.

In describing religious violence, many analysts comment on the importance of phenomena associated with nation-building as factors differentiating contemporary cases from earlier ones. The efforts of many peoples, or at least of elite parties within specific groups, to build states able to wield political and economic power seem to create a mood in which group feeling takes on a militant, mass-organizational character that is unprecedented in the history of many religious traditions. Such feeling can be related positively to nation-building, as peoples seek to assert their claims to dominance within particular territories. It can also be connected with active resistance to the development of national polities, particularly on the part of those placed in the status of minorities by an elite group working to develop a homogeneous national consciousness.

Thus, conflicts in former Yugoslavia, Sudan, Sri Lanka, and in Armenia and Azerbaijan are complicated by the demographic results of state-sponsored population relocation programs. In each case such programs are (or were) an aspect of state strategies to develop industry, reclaim land for agricultural purposes, or re-organize demographic realities in particular territories. In each case one result has been increased tensions between those relocated and more long-standing residents of the areas in question.

Programs of economic development and reform have attained similar results. It is interesting, for example, that some commentators depict Serb-Croat-Muslim hostilities as a conflict between urban and rural sectors of the population.[1] Cities, having received special attention under the Tito regime, are now the object of widespread suspicion and hostility among rural people. The fact that cities such as Belgrade or Sarajevo are also the best examples of the Yugoslav ideal of mixed ethic populations simply deepens rural suspicions, as does the special role of Muslims in the urban centers of Bosnia. In other cases current efforts to reform economies through privatizing selected industries create great tensions, as the presence of foreign investment alters the economic reality in transitional and emerging markets such as those in Eastern Europe and South Asia.

In this regard, it is also worth mentioning the role of communications media, especially video technology. It is a commonplace to say that developments in telecommunications make it difficult for authoritarian regimes to maintain control of information. The role of CNN in the demise of the Soviet Union is cited by some as an important example. Less often noted are the opportunities communications technologies provide to motivate group feeling. In these times, one should note, anyone with a video camera and a little skill can mass-produce a cassette intended to motivate support for the interests of one group over against another. With sponsorship from elite group members, such a relatively low-cost operation can manipulate opinion around the world.[2]

Similarly important is the availability of armaments. Following the Gulf War, much international attention has been focused on state-sponsored programs to develop nuclear weapons, as in the case of North Korea, for example. Even in states not currently developing a nuclear capacity, the availability of sophisticated armaments is an important part of the picture of contemporary conflicts. Less discussed, although even more pervasive, are the efforts of various sub-national groups to arm themselves in order to function as peoples' militias or to fight wars of liberation. As one commentator recently put it, the availability of armaments, coupled with an increase in group feeling, creates situations in which governments no longer rule the streets. Instead, street gangs rule governments. Sinhalese militias, Sudanese popular armies, and Serbian, Croatian, and Muslim forces of irregulars constitute a powerful and ongoing source for the en-

---

[1] A point made in particular by David Steele of the Center for Strategic and International Studies at Georgetown University during oral testimony to the Consulting Group on Religion and the Roots of Conflict.

[2] A point made in particular by Professor Vigen Guroian of Loyola University in Baltimore in his oral testimony to the Consulting Group collaborating on this paper.

actment of religious violence. The existence of this source would be nearly impossible apart from the availability of modern armaments.[1]

CONCLUDING REFLECTIONS ON RELIGION AND VIOLENCE

We could continue to detail the conditions that give contemporary religious violence its special character. Aggressive proselytizing sometimes plays a role, as do authoritarian ideologies and policies that deprive significant populations of basic rights. Further, one cannot ignore the importance of interference by outside powers in certain cases. There are two issues in particular that need attention as we conclude this essay. First: What is it that pushes group differentiation over the edge into violence? One could note cases in which the various patterns indicated—division of the world into "in" and "out" groups, narratives that legitimate those who are "in" and incriminate those who are "out," justifications for resorting to armed force, and the need to dominate within a given territory—can be present without leading to an actual use of armed force. What makes the difference between such cases and those which currently draw our attention? And second: Can religious traditions be part of the solution to, even as they appear to be part of the problem of, religious violence?

As to the first question, we set forth some suggestions advanced in particular by students of the Holocaust.[2] Given the patterns listed above, the presence of "out" groups within the territory to be dominated constitutes a challenge. Some would describe this situation in terms of the creation of cognitive dissonance. The theory of cognitive dissonance, as developed by Leon Festinger and others, may be described as focusing on "the idea that if a person knows various things that are not psychologically consistent with each other, he will in a variety of ways try to make them consistent."[3] Insofar as the domination of an "in" group involves the maintenance of a monopoly on the legitimate exercise of religious

---

[1] For elaboration of these points, see, among others, Stanley Tambiah, "Ethnic Conflict in the World Today," *American Ethnologist* 16/2 (May, 1989): pp. 335-49; see especially pp. 337-39.

[2] See especially the various writings of Richard L. Rubenstein, including *After Auschwitz*, 2nd ed. (Baltimore: John Hopkins University Press, 1992); *Approaches to Auschwitz*, co-authored with John K. Roth (Atlanta: John Knox Press, 1987); and *The Age of Triage* (Boston: Beacon Press, 1983).

[3] Leon Festinger, "Cognitive Dissonance," *Scientific American,* 207 (October, 1962): 93. Festinger further notes that the theory builds on the notion that human beings, as a result of socialization, come to feel that certain ways of thinking, feeling, and behaving "fit" together in what we might call a symbolic world, while others' ways do not. With respect to the Holocaust, the theory of cognitive dissonance is most developed in the works of Richard Rubenstein, cited above.

practice within a given territory, and "out" groups present a distinctive set of practices, the presence of the latter always creates the kind of social-psychological stress described by Festinger. This is particularly the case when "out" group practices present a direct challenge to important components of an "in" group's world view. Students of the Holocaust often note that the continuance of Judaic practices, and thus the presence of Jews as an identifiable people, presented a special challenge to the monopoly of Christianity in Europe. Christianity, in appealing to sources having their origins in Judaic contexts, and in claiming to be the true inheritor of God's promises to Israel, left itself open to challenges from those "left behind"—that is, those basing their legitimacy on a continuity between their practices and those of ancient Israel—namely, the Jewish community. The relationship between Christianity and Judaism illustrates in especially poignant ways the type of tension associated with cognitive dissonance. One should not miss the possibilities of this analytic tool for exploring relationships between other traditions, however: for example, between Christianity and Islam, Islam and indigenous African traditions (especially insofar as the latter may be understood as polytheistic), Sinhalese Buddhists and the mostly Hindu and Muslim Tamils, or between the dominant forms of Christianity in the Americas and the religious traditions of American indigenous peoples.[1] To monopolize the legitimate practice of religion within a given

---

[1] This last relationship provides an especially poignant case, as does the struggle of indigenous peoples in general. Here, an initial military campaign based to some extent on religious factors connected with "in"/"out" group differentiation was followed by attempts to convert or otherwise "civilize" indigenous peoples. Where such peoples resisted conversion and maintained their own traditions with resilience, the dominant culture often resorted to further violence in ways that, in Festinger's terms, suggest an attempt to "try to make [inconsistent things] consistent." An important study of the relations among attempts to civilize indigenous peoples in the United States, indigenous peoples' resistance, and the dominant group's resort to violence may be found in Bernard W. Sheehan, *Seeds of Extinction: Jeffersonian Philanthropy and the American Indian* (Chapel Hill: University of North Carolina Press, 1973). Such tensions remain to this day; one notes the phenomenon described in John Mohawk's "Epilogue" to Paul A.W. Wallace, *White Roots of Peace* (Santa Fe: Clear Light Publishers, 1994), pp. 117-56, whereby the Eisenhower Administration, among others, attempted to eliminate obstacles to particular development projects by "terminating" the legal status of the tribal classification of certain Indian groups. More brutal (though perhaps from the standpoint of indigenous peoples, no more insidious) are the mass killings of indigenous peoples outside the United States: for example, in Guatemala and in the Amazon region of Brazil. See the contribution of Jose Barriero on "Central and South America" in *Voice of Indigenous Peoples* (Santa Fe: Clear Light Publishers, 1994), pp. 127-30. The specific features associated with the phenomenon of cognitive dissonance vary case by case, yet resort to violence and certain other patterns persist in attempts to deal with the social-psychological tensions aroused by the continued existence of an "other." The persistence of these patterns is a striking characteristic of the diverse conflicts with which this essay is concerned.

territory requires the establishment and maintenance of structures suggesting the plausibility of a particular world view. The presence of dissent, when sufficiently strong, tends to weaken these structures.

The key phrase here is "sufficiently strong." Again, some students of the Holocaust suggest that one of the key factors in turning people's suspicion of a Jewish minority into systematic violence was the growing presence of European Jews in positions of influence.[1] If the continued existence of Judaism was troubling to the Christian majority of Europe, the fact that most Jews lived in ghettos designed, built, and administered in ways signifying secondary status nevertheless provided an important reminder of the "triumph" of Christianity. When sufficient numbers of Jews moved out of ghettos and into the mainstream of European political, economic, and especially intellectual life, the Jewish community no longer provided such a ready reinforcement of European Christianity's plausibility structure. In response to the challenges posed by Jews and by Judaism released from ghetto existence, historic fears of this "out" group were magnified. Together with a number of other factors, such alterations in the encounter between Christians and Jews in Europe may help to explain the phenomenon of the Holocaust.

One need not look far for similar dynamics in contemporary conflicts. The presence of "out" groups is always capable of challenging the religious monopoly of an "in" group. In ordinary situations, "in" groups address this challenge in a variety of ways, each of which may be seen as an attempt to deal with a situation of cognitive dissonance: for example, attempts to convert members of the "out" group and public policies crafted as reminders of a group's second-class status.[2] The more resistant and resilient an "out" group is, the more important or influential members of the "out" group become, and the more direct (and therefore threatening) the challenge to the plausibility structures that support "in" group monopoly. If the threat is perceived as strong enough, at least some factions within the "in" group may be expected to resort to or to promote violence as a response.

---

[1] Not that "strength" need always have this character. One could imagine situations in which demographic considerations in and of themselves might be the factor that pushes groups toward violence.

[2] It seems important to stress in this connection that strategies of conversion and the like may be viewed as coming from the same root as religious violence. If one considers cognitive dissonance in the manner outlined above, even peaceable efforts at conversion may be seen as an attempt to limit or to eliminate the power of "out" groups. From the standpoint of human rights norms and instruments, violent strategies, including war, genocide, forced conversions, and forced migration, pose special problems. However, even peaceful efforts to convert an "out" group can share the motive of reducing dissonance, particularly when such efforts enjoy support from governments.

As to the issue pertaining to positive resources in religious traditions for dealing with conflict, another paper in this collection has primary responsibility for identifying these resources. Our task has been to pose the problematic role of religion in contemporary conflicts. We have tried to do so as starkly as possible because of the seriousness of the problem of religious violence in our day. With respect to solutions, we note only the following:

(1) **Religious solutions to the problems of religious violence must address the same social and psychological needs that contemporary militant formulations of religious traditions address.** The desire for a secure place in the universe, which religious traditions address in the creation of group feeling, cannot be ignored; neither can it be redirected in ways that serve intercommunal peace without serious attempts to address the psychological, social, and political needs that attend this desire.

Furthermore, any serious attempt to deal with religious violence must find or develop the full range of ways to express sacred values. That is, it must move beyond interpretations of sacred scriptures that support toleration or examinations of the history of traditions in order to challenge the rightness of militant doctrinal formulations. As noted above, religious traditions promote group feeling through a range of practices, including rituals and, very significantly in many modern conflicts, recitation of narratives that legitimate "in" group distinctiveness and incriminate various "out" groups. An attempt to identify religious resources for dealing with the roots of conflict must look for ways to turn narratives of conflict into narratives that promote the type of mutual respect and tolerance envisioned in human rights instruments. Moreover, one cannot ignore the role of charismatic leadership in religious traditions, a leadership that can serve as a catalyst either for violence, or for peace.

(2) **An attempt to address religious violence in the long run must take account of the ways contemporary conflicts are likely to be the seedbed for the conflicts of the future.** Most analyses of former Yugoslavia, for example, note that as the war drags on, the relative liberalism of Bosnia's Muslims is rapidly turning in the direction of more militant expressions of group sentiment. In this case, as in others, we are reminded that oppression yields oppression, and fundamentalisms breed fundamentalisms.

(3) **An attempt to develop the resources of religious traditions against religious violence must deal with the phenomenon which some have termed the "reemergence of history" in the late 20th century.** By this term, we are reminded that for many peoples history has been on hold for a significant portion of this century. Under Soviet dominance or colonial or post-colonial rule, such peoples perceived themselves to be in a situation that threatened their very survival. In these situations, the development and recitation of religio-historical

narratives—often, it should be said, "behind closed doors" as part of resistance movements—were perhaps *the* most important factors in preserving group identity. In post-Cold War and post-colonialist contexts, such groups now feel impelled to renew their historic quests for goals beyond survival. They are ready to build, to preach, and to conquer. Historical goals, now pursued with a militancy and mass-organizational character born of the modern ideology of nationalism, are supported by new communications and weapons technologies, and they are fostered by the complications of trying to build modern economies for modern states. Part of the irony of contemporary religious conflict is that religious factors in group life are at one and the same time among the most constructive and the most destructive forces in human affairs.

The initial and final versions of this paper were drafted by Charles B. Strozier. The consultation with other members of the Consultation Group on Religious Militancy or "Fundamentalism" consisted of lengthy taped interviews with Robert Jay Lifton and Veena Oldenburg, telephone interviews with Leila Ahmed and Jack Hawley, and a paper submitted by Samuel Heilman (after some conversations). In the interviews and in Heilman's paper, the members of the Consultation Group responded to a series of questions devised by Strozier. Michael Flynn at the Center on Violence and Human Survival, John Jay College, CUNY, also contributed many useful ideas. The members of the other Consultation Groups whose work appears in this publication all contributed to this process as well in the planning meetings organized by the Project on Religion and Human Rights. Special thanks should be given to David Little, Stanley Tambiah, Abdullahi An-Na'im, Ann Elizabeth Mayer, Arvind Sharma, and Harvey Cox. At these meetings (and in other conversations), both Paul Moore, Jr. and Kusumita Pedersen offered many ideas for this paper. In the process of final revision, the suggestions and editing of John Kelsay and Sumner B. Twiss were invaluable.

2

Religious Militancy
or "Fundamentalism"

Many disparate and relatively new forms of religious militancy around the world threaten the human rights of individuals and groups. In some cases, religious fanatics actually commit violence to further their sacred agenda, as they understand it. More generally, these "fundamentalists" change the debate among the faithful themselves over the role of religion in the family and in public life. Fundamentalists insist they are maintaining an unbroken tradition, although they are, in fact, transforming that tradition. Their basic goal is to fight back—culturally, ideologically, and socially—against the assumptions and patterns of life that are taken for granted in contemporary secular society and culture, refusing to celebrate them or to embrace them fully. They keep their distance and refuse to endorse the legitimacy of any culture that opposes what they perceive as fundamental truths. Secular culture, in their eyes, is base, barbarous, crude, and essentially profane. It produces a society that respects no sacred order and ignores the possibility of redemption.

"Fundamentalism," however, is a troubling term for many scholars and religious believers. Given its association in the media with violence and fanaticism, it is often avoided as a term of self-designation by those whom one might be otherwise be tempted to identify as fundamentalists. At the same time, the fundamentalist label is virtually unavoidable if one wishes to speak about various contemporary movements which, despite their differences, share significant resemblances. The problems associated with the label are clear. If, for example, textual literalism works as a shared defining criterion for fundamentalist movements within Christianity, Judaism, and Islam, it has little relevance in Hinduism. Furthermore, only Christians are "reborn," and by no means are all such believers necessarily fundamentalists. One vital aspect of Christian fundamentalism is its apocalyptic orientation, although Muslim and Hindu "fundamentalists" are primarily concerned with the religious transformation of civil society in the contemporary world, and many people, especially in the United States, are apocalyptic without being fundamentalist.

At the same time, one can identify common sources of fundamentalism. Psychologically, for example, fundamentalisms emerge out of concerns for normative values when something threatens the very essence of the self in the life-death continuum. Such threats are a necessary prelude to religious *or* political fundamentalism, and they set the stage for a group purifying process that can become genocidal in the designation of the "Other" as evil.

Part of the definitional problem is that the term "fundamentalism" is closely associated with Christianity ideologically, theologically, and historically. The word "fundamentalism" was first used in 1920 as a call to arms for the faithful. It named a loose movement within Christianity that had been taking shape in the previous half-century. It is a term firmly grounded in the ideological developments of the 19th century (especially in John Nelson Darby's theory of premillennial dispensationalism, the key ideas of which date from the 1830s). The term was shaped in the crisis of the Civil War and found its crucial concept in the principle of biblical inerrancy developed at Princeton Theological Seminary in the 1880s. This concept forged a long Christian tradition of literalism into dogma. But it was not until the mid-20th century that a *mass movement* of *fundamentalism* took shape. Fundamentalism became then a loosely allied group of fiercely believing Christians who are "born again" and evangelical, believe broadly in inerrancy, and eagerly await the imminent return of Jesus. These "fundamentalists" are mostly Southern Baptists, conservative evangelicals, and Pentecostals, although many would sharply distinguish between Pentecostals and "fundamentalists."

For often quite different but seemingly analogous reasons, there has been a marked increase of fundamentalist-like believers in other world religions on all continents since at least the mid-20th century. At present "fundamentalism" is a troubling but unavoidable term under which people currently put together a number of movements arising out of disparate conditions yet sharing certain features. In lieu of a definition of fundamentalism, certain characteristics common to all fundamentalisms can be noted. As Martin Marty has pointed out, fundamentalists in general are *not* just conservative, traditional, or orthodox. Fundamentalism is not fossilized or static but alive and dynamic; not generically based in biblical inerrancy or indeed even in literalism; and not the only possible departure from mainstream faiths (another example of departure is New Age religion). Fundamentalists are not anti-scientific or anti-rational (at least in their own view) and certainly not anti-technological; not declining in influence; not always militant; and not always poor or uneducated. What they *are* is reactive against many aspects of modern life, e.g., its pluralism, consumerism, materialism, and stress on the equality of men and women. Fundamentalists selectively choose certain normative "fundamentals" that define their faith and lives, while they oppose any spiritualization of teachings or metaphoric interpretations of sacred texts. Such an approach makes them exclusivist and separatist. They are also absolutist. They have no room for ambiguity or relativism, which tends to make them authoritarian. In ethics they are uniformly anti-permissive, particularly in matters of sexuality and of the role of women in society. They also see themselves as agents of the sacred, as actors in God's cosmic drama, which makes them deeply teleological. History has a purpose. Nothing is random.[1]

Perhaps fundamentalism is as much a state of mind as an orientation to a specific religious tradition. It may be part of a general response to "proteanism," the psychological openness and sense of experimentation, ambiguity, and ethical relativism that have come to define the experience of the self in advanced technological societies. Fundamentalists contend mightily with proteanism, yet they are never still or static in their dynamic relationship with it. They have shown themselves, for example, to be masters of combining modern technology with pursuit of their anti-modern project. Fundamentalist goals can almost certainly never be achieved, for they are decidedly utopian and run counter to some three centuries of firmly ingrained traditions of human rights and democracy. But fundamentalists themselves can cause much mischief. Their systems are totalistic and tend to turn purifying impulses into absolutist terms, which makes their beliefs unrealizable, but also all the more potent. The systems call forth energy.

THE APPEAL OF FUNDAMENTALISM

Among those who embrace the contemporary world and view it in a generally positive light, there is a tacit assumption that with time, things generally get better. There is such a thing as progress, they say; the new *is* improved, and today is superior to yesterday. The movement of civilization is always forward. The harshness of early existence has been replaced by an increasingly amelio-

---

[1] Martin Marty, "Fundamentalism as a Social Phenomenon," *Bulletin of The American Academy of Arts and Sciences* 42 (1988): pp. 15-29. There are, of course, other definitions and emphases in the volumes of the "The Fundamentalism Project" [Martin E. Marty and R. Scott Appleby, eds., (Chicago: University of Chicago Press, 1991-1994)]. To date four volumes have been published: *Fundamentalisms Observed*, *Fundamentalisms and Society*, *Fundamentalisms and the State*, and *Accounting for Fundamentalisms*. Two additional volumes, which are forthcoming, will complete the series.

rated condition. That is, life since the beginning of recorded history has been a climb out of darkness into light. Socially, the individual gradually has been freed from the bonds of ascribed status and allowed to make of himself or herself what he or she wills. Merit rather than birth, social station, ethnicity, religion, or race is to be the vehicle of individual success or failure, while democracy and freedom replace autocracy and servitude.

Fundamentalists earnestly oppose these comfortable assumptions. Individuality is seen not as liberation but rather as a recipe for loneliness and alienation. Liberation from tradition is not understood as freedom but instead as an erosion of sacred order and a decline in moral standards. Democracy is understood to be ruled by the lowest common denominator and standards. At best, democracy is seen to be misguided because it lacks fundamental religious direction and values. Science and technology are not viewed as blessings but rather are perceived to have run amok, enabling human beings to act irresponsibly, to destroy life through, for example, nuclear war or abortion, or to manipulate life in mindless madness. Most of those who view science and technology with such reservations continue, however, to use them to improve their material conditions. For example, they use modern medicine to heal themselves and use satellite broadcasts to radiate their messages far and wide. Yet they generally refuse to endow either science or technology with any transcendent meaning or moral legitimacy; achievements of science and technology are never presented as worthwhile goals of life but only as useful means for sustaining it.

Fundamentalism stresses the need to be part of a community of like-minded believers who share a set of practices, allegiances, and lifestyles. In some cases communities may go so far as to prescribe garb, diets, and addresses. Generally, fundamentalism stresses a common educational system. Such cultural and social intimacy stands in sharp contrast to the impersonal relations that appear to define the society of unbelievers. If nothing else, fundamentalists experience a solidarity with those who share in their "struggle" against the retrograde forces of secular society. They also may share in the psychological rewards of being part of a movement of restoration that, they believe, will survive the vicissitudes of history. Thus they can handle the loss of a battle here or there because they remain convinced that they will ultimately win the war; this is no small part of the appeal of fundamentalism. Moreover, all it takes to share in this feeling of triumph is a commitment to faith and to sacred order. To Christians realization of this commitment may mean being "born again," to Jews being a "ba'al t'shuvah" or a returnee to the ways of the faith, to Muslims embracing the Islamic revival, and to members of other religions a similar personal acceptance of a "truth" and a public identification with a community of believers. Fundamentalisms offer persons an anchor in history and a sense of identity.

The appeal of fundamentalism, however, can also be direct and pragmatic. In the Islamic world, fundamentalists often provide the best and most important social services. In Egypt, for example, they operate free clinics that are much better run and more accessible than those supported by the government. During the recent earthquakes in Cairo, it was the fundamentalists who put up tents and provided direct assistance to thousands suddenly made homeless. Fundamentalists also provide a wide range of services to help the city's rural migrants. Much more than the government, which many regard as distant, insensitive, and corrupt, the fundamentalists seem to be aware of people's needs.

African-American forms of fundamentalism are similarly characterized by a mixture of strident and pragmatic behaviors. A black, independent Pentecostal congregation in Harlem, for example, is fundamentalist in its formal belief structures and proclaims itself an "end time church with an end time mission." Newcomers to the church are required to attend classes on "premillennial dispensationalism." A marked literalism governs the approach to the Bible. Notions such as that of tribulation and the rapture are in the air, and the apocalyptic idea of human history ending and Jesus soon returning haunts church rituals and sermons. There is even a "shadow side" to the church in its intolerance of homosexuals. But in other respects, this remarkable church is the only vital, ongoing institution in the deeply troubled surrounding community. Its activities include soup kitchens, anti-drug programs, and outreach to adolescents. It at least touches politics in angry attempts to preserve the neighborhood for blacks and stave off the onslaught of more economically advantaged white New Yorkers eager for apartment space. As the charismatic pastor of the church put it during one interview, "If I hadn't become a preacher, I would have been a revolutionary."

More typically, fundamentalism is the voice of right wing and reactionary political dissent. The Christian Coalition in America aspires to take control of the Republican party and to create a kind of proto-theocratic state. In many Middle Eastern countries and on the Indian subcontinent, fundamentalism is in a very real sense political. From Hamas in the West Bank and Gaza to radical Islam in Algiers to the Bharatiya Janata Party (BJP) in India, fundamentalism cannot be separated from politics. To the extent that democracy exists at all in the developed world, it is seen as an alien and foreign product of colonial domination. It is perceived, with a good deal of truth, to be a means used by the elites to hold on to their power and to perpetuate the unequal distribution of resources in society. Many fundamentalists feel the only way to "fight back" is to turn to a new form of religious militancy and then seize the reins of government.

FUNDAMENTALISM AND HUMAN RIGHTS

Because their greatest allegiance is to their beliefs and faith communities, fundamentalists necessarily look upon all else as secondary. Nonbelievers are at best pitiable and at worst cultural adversaries. In no sense are nonbelievers innocents. Even if all they do is to live their own lives in ways that demonstrate a contempt for, or at least a denial of, the fundamental truths, they are viewed as embodiments of heresy. At best they are to be ignored or repudiated. At worst they are to be obliterated and destroyed so that they do not contaminate the ontologically and culturally superior way of life or those who are its innocent believers, primarily the young (and as yet unsullied). Fundamentalists claim to be protecting the young above all others. The quest for purity and purification in the spiritual realm can be regenerative, although it may also result in deadly totalism.

In general, it would seem that for fundamentalists human rights must be founded in and integrated with notions of divine and/or communal rights. Apart from such integration, claims for individual human rights may appear as an insidious insinuation of cultural pluralism and of religious or moral relativism. As Rabbi Shimon Schwab has written, "Sometimes *emet* [truth] takes top priority, even if it means reducing the level of *shalom* [peace]."[1] Human rights may bring peace, but the fundamentalist believes truth, based on divinely ordained obligations, must carry the day. Therefore, those who want to share in "rights" must share in the obligations that God has placed upon human creatures. Furthermore, in the fundamentalist view, to be a human being is not to be just any sort of person but rather to be one who has accepted the word and teachings of the divine and of those who interpret the divine word and follow the divine ways. Other people are infidels, heretics, and enemies. In the battle for redemption, nonbelievers have lost in a very real sense something crucial in their status as human beings. To be fully human one must believe.

The pluralism of democracy undermines these commitments and can generate terrifying violence in situations of political strife. Consider the example of Hebron. The Book of Exodus says that Amalek must be wiped from the earth. Moreover, even the memory of Amalek must be wiped out, for "the Lord will have war with Amalek from generation to generation" (17:16). This belief undoubtedly was on Baruch Goldstein's mind when he started shooting in the Hebron mosque on Purim, the Jewish holiday traditionally associated with victory over Amalek.

---

[1] Shimon Schwab, *Selected Writings* (Lakewood, NJ: C.I.S. Publications, 1988), pp. 315-16.

In Islam contradictions can arise from the association of democracy with colonialism. Certainly, many of those who are part of the Islamic revival are intolerant of dissent, deviance, and disorder. It is also true that fundamentalism gives a greater share of power in the family and in culture at large to men over against women.[1] But the (re)veiling of women, especially in Egypt, has been specifically called for by some educated women, including university students and professionals. Many of these women find a kind of liberation in the ways that veiling covers their role in the public space. In Egypt, at least, there can be an overlap between the Islamic revival and female self-assertion.[2]

In Christianity the fundamentalist movement is deeply divided between the ideologues in places such as Dallas Theological Seminary or Bob Jones University, on the one hand, and the loose apocalypticism and belief systems of many Pentecostals. The latter (if indeed one identifies them as part of the "family" of fundamentalists) bring to their religious practice a spontaneity and to their beliefs a refreshing uncertainty, tending to soften the harsher edges of their dogma. Their deepest commitments can connect with many goals of the human rights community that promote justice.

On the other hand, fundamentalists of all stripes tend to be exclusionist and authoritarian, and the edges of the movement can be very odd (e.g., the community in Waco or the Christian Identity groups).[3] Children raised in fundamentalist families and churches often seem to carry a large psychological burden. In the

---

[1] Perhaps this is the place to mention that there is some evidence of gender-specific differences among fundamentalists. Male fundamentalists, for example, often project harsh images of end-time destruction, appear to be rigidly puritanical regarding relations between the sexes, and emphasize self-control over potentially dangerous desires and passions. Women fundamentalists, by contrast, tend to have more gentle images of the end time, preferring to focus on positive conceptions of the millennium, and, while certainly oriented to conventional and patriarchally influenced role models (e.g., the dutiful wife), appear less concerned about controlling contrary desires and more interested in emphasizing images of love and care in personal relationships. Given the recent work of feminist moral psychologists and philosophers, these findings on gender differences are hardly surprising, but they are nonetheless pertinent to a fuller understanding of the phenomenon of fundamentalism. For further work on this issue, see Charles B. Strozier, *Apocalypse: On the Psychology of Fundamentalism in America* (Boston: Beacon Press, 1994), pp. 124-29; also see note 8, pp. 265-66.

[2] This particular paradoxical result should not be taken to indicate that Islamic fundamentalism is not significantly patriarchal and therefore in serious tension with women's efforts the world over to gain a more powerful civil and political voice. In other contexts, (re)veiling by Muslim women is better interpreted as an operational concession to a powerful patriarchal system--that is, a tactic of survival in what is, by human rights standards, an oppressive environment.

[3] Michael Barkun, *Religion and the Racist Right: The Origins of the Christian Identity Movement* (Chapel Hill, NC: The University of North Carolina Press, 1994).

interest of fulfilling their role in history, fundamentalists would deny others the pursuit of different goals.

They can be unsteady, these Christian fundamentalists, and their apocalyptic commitments undermine their attachment to the institutions and traditions of law and freedom in, for example, the United States. And the *theological* violence of some forms of fundamentalism is disturbing. In these forms the locus of agency is shifted, which has important psychological consequences and numbs awareness, for it is God, in anger at human failings, who brings on the destruction. In a kind of theistic genocide, the fundamentalists' God makes "blood run up to the bridles of horses" and "turns rivers red." Ultimate violence cleanses and purifies. The violence is everywhere, and it is total. In the end, not one nonbeliever is spared. For some, the war of God redeems and sanctifies, but in the process this fragile human experiment we have *must* be violently and completely destroyed.

WHAT IS TO BE DONE

It would be facile to imagine that there are any easy solutions to problems in the complex interactions between fundamentalism and human rights. The political, social, and religious contexts in which fundamentalism flourishes vary considerably. In much of the non-Western world, there is a general sense that the West has failed and now needs to acknowledge the ways in which its actions have fueled fundamentalisms around the world. If there were something approaching a more equitable distribution of the world's resources, fundamentalisms would significantly diminish. Western export of its aggressive market economies that disproportionately reward the richer northern hemisphere bears a heavy responsibility for current forms of religious militancy from northern Africa to the Middle East to the Indian subcontinent.

There are, however, more proximate levels at which solutions can be sought. Everyone needs education in the more complex and humane dimensions of his or her own religious tradition. Only if people in general are religiously literate can they combat the simplicities and generalizations upon which many fundamentalisms build their arguments. Religions are far more complex and multivocal than they appear to be in the presentations of most fundamentalists. Traditions often contain within themselves a variety of realities; minority and majority opinions exist beside one another, and many faith traditions abide within the major traditions. Various perspectives offer a richness to religious behavior and spiritual life that is covered over by the broad brush strokes of fundamentalism. Only by insuring that people are fully informed of the many facets of a religion can we combat the monolithic perspectives of fundamentalism. Human rights advocates have an interest in supporting religious education of the widest and deepest sort. Leaders with the goal of providing a complete and complex religious training need support. Those who sponsor publication of the texts of particular traditions should be encouraged to include examples of all points of view, not just the texts that the current purveyors of a fundamentalist interpretation have selectively retrieved and rendered relevant. Religious education is too important to be left only in the hands of the fundamentalists.

Equally pragmatically, different *kinds* of human rights need to be distinguished in descriptions of the encounter between fundamentalisms and religion. The preservation and protection of life is not a principle that is antithetical to fundamentalism. Militant religious movements of all kinds easily can be imagined as reinforcing the core human rights values that deplore war and genocide. This intersection of basic principles has potentially far-reaching consequences for the human rights community's future effectiveness in many troubled areas of the world.[1]

Many fundamentalist movements (although not, on the whole, those of white Christians) are deeply committed to advancing ways of meeting people's material needs for nutrition, housing, medical care, and other social services. Such commitments position many militant religious movements ambiguously, and positively from a human rights standpoint, in relation to social and economic human rights. The goal, it would seem, in this regard is to build alliances around

---

[1] Interestingly, a number of Native American indigenous traditions can be interpreted as manifesting certain features, as described in this essay, that are characteristic of fundamentalism. Indigenous religious cultures, too, are not just traditional and conservative, but alive and dynamic. They are not based in literalism, for their traditions and scriptures are oral. They are not anti-scientific or anti-rational, for they are open to aligning traditional practices (e.g., curing ceremonies) with the benefits of modern science (e.g., medicine). But, like other fundamentalists, they are reactive against many aspects of modern, secular life in the dominant culture, such as consumerism, certain uses of applied technology deemed threatening to ecosystems, and abortion on demand. Moreover, the societal values and practices of such traditions are deeply communitarian, and a number of their world views are significantly teleological, if not apocalyptic. Consider, for example, the Hopi prophecy of the "Great Purification" if all peoples do not return to life in harmony with nature (see Thomas Banyacya, "Address to the United Nations" in Alexander Ewen, ed., *Voice of Indigenous Peoples: Native People Address the United Nations* (Santa Fe: Clear Light Publishers, 1994), pp. 112-18.

At the same time, it is important to note that indigenous traditions are *not* militant in ways often associated with the label "fundamentalist." These traditions stand for peace and indeed seem quite open to meshing their communitarian orientation with international human rights agendas. An example of such intersection can be found in the United Nations Draft Declaration on Indigenous Peoples Rights (see Ewen, pp. 159-74). The luminous fact that certain apparently fundamentalist traditions are from many Native American perspectives compatible with the recognition of and respect for human rights provides hope that other fundamentalisms also can come to appreciate that they need not be antagonistic to human rights.

fundamentalist critiques of existing regimes. These regimes have far too often created and maintained large gaps between rich and poor and have failed to provide needy people with important social services.

Other kinds of human rights that touch social, familial, and even political values and practices operate at a different level of moral and conceptual meaning. In those arenas conflict is more likely, and a common purpose is extremely problematic. The scale of difference between genocide, war, and torture, on the one hand, and (re)veiling of women, the right to form unions, and a free press, on the other, is profound. With regard to the former, there may be considerable agreement between fundamentalists and nonfundamentalists alike on the prohibition of such practices. With respect to the latter, fundamentalists' commitments in these social and political, but especially familial, areas may be deep and abiding. These commitments also are likely to be significantly different from the commitments of nonfundamentalists and the human rights community. Perhaps the human rights community needs to shape its agenda with greater awareness to the possible in areas of fundamentalist influence. On the other hand, for many contemporary rights activists to relinquish the sense of urgency in reforming the social, political, and familial arrangements in much of the world would run counter to their most passionate commitments.

Finally, what most of all nourishes fundamentalism in Christianity, and perhaps in other religions as well, is the lack of faith among ordinary people in a human future. Wars, genocide, and nuclear weapons undermine such faith. With faith that human life will continue, perhaps Christian fundamentalists will turn to the truer sources of Christianity in the Sermon on the Mount and away from obsessions with the Book of Revelation; Jews from *haredi* commitments to the ambiguities and humanism of a tradition that embraces Isaiah and Job, as well as Moses and Abraham; Muslims to the *jihad* as a process of self-discovery and away from "holy war" and imposition of a harsh version of the *shari'a*; and Hindus to the wonderful contradictions of Shiva. Peace and justice, and perhaps only peace and justice, will convince fundamentalists to live peaceably with other humane images of God and of utopia.

This paper is very much a group project, consisting of insight, information, and formulation provided by all members of the Consultation Group on Universality vs. Relativism in Human Rights: Abdullahi A. An-Na'im (Chair of the Consultation Group), Executive Director, Human Rights Watch/Africa; Ann Elizabeth Mayer, Associate Professor of Legal Studies, Wharton School, Unversity of Pennsylvania; Sumner B. Twiss, Professor of Religious Studies and Department Chair, Brown University; William Wipfler, Anglican Observer, United Nations (retired), and former Director, Human Rights Office of the National Council of Churches. Although Sumner Twiss served as principal coordinating author of this paper's drafts, it must be clearly understood that the final document includes many paragraphs originally written by Abdullahi An-Na'im and Ann Mayer. Especially important to the conceptualization and production of this paper was the creative tension generated by the differing perspectives of group members. Useful critical commentary on the first draft of the paper was additionally provided by the executive staff of the Project on Religion and Human Rights, especially Kusumita P. Pedersen, Executive Director, and Bishop Paul Moore, Jr., Co-Chair of the Project, the Chairs of the three other Consultation Groups associated with the Project; Robert Traer, General Secretary of the International Association for Religious Freedom (Oxford, England); two faculty colleagues, Wendell Dietrich and Giles Milhaven, and four Ph.D. candidates in the Department of Religious Studies, Brown University, Tracy Coleman, David Fryer, James Gubbins, and Mark Hadley. Special thanks are due to Tracy Coleman and Wendell Dietrich for reviewing the second draft on short notice. Ann Mayer's contributions to the final draft were invaluable. We also wish to acknowledge the excellent labors of Kathleen Pappas, Coordinating Secretary (in charge of faculty manuscripts production), Department of Religious Studies, Brown University.

3

Universality vs. Relativism in Human Rights

It is an undeniable fact that Western cultural influences shaped the 1948 Universal Declaration of Human Rights and have continued to affect the formulation of subsequent international human rights covenants.[1] Awareness of these influences, among other factors, has resulted in ideological conflict on the international scene involving challenges to the universal applicability of human rights, as well as denials that human rights norms can or should be conceived as timeless and uncontestable standards of human behavior applicable to all nations. Such challenges and denials are often advanced in the form of claims about diversity and relativism among the world's philosophical, religious, and cultural traditions.[2] To what extent are these challenges, denials, and claims credible? Do they simply represent a smokescreen for the perpetration and perpetuation of human rights abuses? Do they represent a genuine tension between the international legal system of universal human rights, on the one hand, and particular moral and cultural traditions, on the other? And, if there is a tension, can it be resolved or mitigated in a way that advances human rights for oppressed persons and peoples?

Other undeniable facts are also relevant to these issues. For example, in the nearly fifty years since the Universal Declaration was adopted, the influence of non-Western countries on the formulation of subsequent international human

---

[1] For the texts of these documents, see *Human Rights: The International Bill of Human Rights* (New York: United Nations, 1993), which includes the Universal Declaration of Human Rights, the International Covenant on Economic, Social and Cultural Rights, and the International Covenant on Civil and Political Rights and Optional Protocols.

[2] These denials and challenges have been exacerbated by recent misleading discourse about the coming clash of civilizations and cultures in the arena of global politics; see, e.g., Samuel Huntington, "The Clash of Civilizations?" *Foreign Affairs* (Summer 1993): pp. 22-49.

rights covenants and treaties has increased to the point where newly formulated human rights, as well as new human rights priorities, have been recognized by the international community—e.g., communal rights to self-determination and development, so-called "green rights," and increasingly emphasized social and economic rights. Moreover, it seems clear that Western perspectives on, and thinking about, human rights have been evolving in such a way that the West can no longer be regarded as a homogenous cultural tradition solely interested in civil and political rights to the relative exclusion of social, cultural, and economic rights.[1] Inasmuch as these trends suggest that cultural influence is a two-way street, might there be a rapprochement between universal human rights and particular cultural traditions that is ultimately beneficial to oppressed groups and people? Do these trends suggest that, despite their predominantly Western origins, human rights can nonetheless be (re)formulated so as to be sufficiently responsive to the legitimate insights and needs of non-Western cultural traditions? Is it really the case that the concept of universal human rights is in necessary tension with cultural traditions, or can such universality be accommodated by all traditions in a manner that would enhance recognition and compliance with human rights standards?

What seems clear at this historical moment is that there is a widespread perception on the part of many that the present normative notion of universal human rights is in tension with moral and cultural diversity in the world.[2] This perception, however, needs to be scrutinized critically in order to determine whether it is well-founded or, for example, simply stems from uncritical acceptance of the political manipulations of the language of moral diversity and relativism by certain governments that want to shield themselves from criticism (and possible intervention) by the international community for ongoing human rights violations. Such manipulations must be distinguished from sincere efforts

---

[1] This perceptive observation is made by Virginia A. Leary in her important article, "The Effect of Western Perspectives on International Human Rights" in Abdullahi A. An-Na'im and F. Deng, eds., *Human Rights in Africa: Cross-Cultural Perspectives* (Washington, D. C.: Brookings Institution, 1990), pp. 15-30; see especially pp. 17 and 25. This introduction is much indebted to Leary's insights and arguments. It seems important to observe that the West has tended to give priority to civil-political human rights over socio-economic human rights, even when societies and cultures outside the West have articulated their moral perception that socio-economic rights are at least as important as civil and political rights. Fortunately, this tendency is now being countervailed by calls to (re)affirm the indivisibility of these two types of human rights; on this point, see, e.g., Philip Alston, "Human Rights in 1993: How Far Has the United Nations Come and Where Should It Go From Here?" (unpublished typescript).

[2] For a vivid example of this perception, see Alison Renteln, *International Human Rights: Universalism Versus Relativism* (New York: Sage Publications, 1990). See also Adamantia Pollis and Petra Schwab, eds., *Human Rights: Cultural and Ideological Perspectives* (New York: Praeger, 1979).

by nongovernmental organizations (NGOs), religious leaders, and private individuals to examine critically and constructively possible tensions between the universality of human rights and strongly imbedded cultural-moral beliefs and practices.

The purpose of this paper is twofold. We wish, first, to outline certain dimensions of the debate about universality vs. relativism in human rights discourse, in the hope of offering a useful diagnosis of certain underlying factors. Second, we will propose a three-pronged strategy for resolving, or at least tempering, this debate, a strategy that involves elements of self-criticism, recognition of crucial premises, and multi-level dialogues about human rights norms and issues.

DIAGNOSIS OF FACTORS IN THE DEBATE

For reasons of organization and clarity, we identify three broad and fundamental dimensions of the debate over universality vs. relativism in human rights: (1) levels of discourse, (2) perspectives of speakers, and (3) cultural complexity. Each of these dimensions involves a number of distinctive elements and issues.

Levels of Discourse

Human rights have both legal and moral dimensions that correlate roughly with a distinction, and possible tension, between the universality of international human rights and the diversity of moral-cultural traditions. The universality of international human rights principles set forth in the Universal Declaration and other components of the International Bill of Human Rights is, legally speaking, a given. Human rights law is extensively elaborated and codified in international treaties and is also supported by customary international law. In theory, this law is both uniform and definite; there is no gainsaying its universal intent, scope, and application. However, pressures to allow culture-based deviations from international human rights norms have grown. These pressures recently culminated, for example, in efforts by many Asian and Muslim states at the 1993 World Conference on Human Rights in Vienna to challenge the universality of human rights principles as they are currently set out in international law and to seek modification of these principles on the grounds that they are too ethnocentrically Western. The final conference declaration proclaims with deliberate ambiguity that human rights are universal in nature but that regional differences, as well as historical, cultural, and religious backgrounds, should be taken into account.[1]

At the moral level, the dimensions of human rights have never been as uniform and definite as they are in international law. This fact correlates with moral-cultural diversity, under which religious diversity may be subsumed.[2] The fact of diversity at the moral-cultural level is reinforced by the further consideration that the Enlightenment-oriented reasoning often used to articulate and to justify the scope and content of human rights standards is not globally accepted and is not persuasive to everyone in many cultures, including Western cultures. Moreover, there is an increasing awareness around the world that moral norms and modes of both reasoning and evaluation are significantly conditioned by historical and cultural contexts.

These various moral and legal considerations appear, at least in theory, to generate a significant tension between, on the one hand, claims about the universality of human rights standards, and, on the other, the evident moral diversity among cultural traditions, especially when these traditions are committed to different philosophical and religious premises and understandings of person and society. The problem is this: Speaking normatively, human rights ought to be, by definition, universal in content, scope, and application; they should constitute a globally accepted set of moral and legal claims to which all human beings are entitled by virtue of their humanity and without distinction. Yet the meaning and implications of specific human rights norms are, arguably, conditioned by the historical and cultural experiences of human societies and traditions. Therefore, it would seem that the articulation and implementation of such norms in concrete situations would be specific to a given human society in its own time and place. By the same token, a moral system appropriate to one society might not be (entirely) appropriate to other societies, which might need to elaborate their own systems from their respective historical and cultural circumstances. But, then, this recognition seems to make it somewhat paradoxical to speak of the universal validity of any given set of human rights standards: whence the tension.

---

[1] The text of this declaration is available in *World Conference on Human Rights: The Vienna Declaration and Programme of Action June 1993* (New York: United Nations, 1993).

[2] At this point it seems appropriate to note our preference for using the language of "cultural" and "cultural traditions" instead of "religious" and "religions" because of the difficulty of distinguishing in precise ways moral, religious, philosophical, and cultural factors. We stipulate for the purposes of this paper that "cultural" is to include all such factors. For a contrasting view that seeks greater precision in the definition of basic terms, see David Little and Sumner B. Twiss, *Comparative Religious Ethics: A New Method* (San Fransisco: Harper & Row, 1978), chs. 1-4.

Some may try to suggest that this tension invalidates the universality of human rights. We do not agree with this position for a number of reasons. No persuasive case has yet been made to show that the tension, in either theory or practice, is not resolvable. Moreover, human rights set aspirational norms, and no persuasive case has been made to show that universal human rights conceived as a goal is either illegitimate or unattainable. Furthermore, recognition of a possible tension between universality and relativism with regard to certain contestable human rights norms must not overlook the fact that many other human rights norms are regarded as universal and uncontestable by the world's moral-cultural traditions. In addition, one needs to acknowledge the fact that many states have, in fact, ratified legally binding universal human rights instruments. The tension, then, poses a practical problem, but it does not imply moral bankruptcy. It calls not for the rejection of universal human rights standards, but rather for the development of creative moral strategies for universalizing such standards which acknowledge and engage seriously the cultural perspectives of traditions committed to diverse premises and world views.

To understand the nature of the universality vs. relativism debate and to understand how religions relate to human rights, one must sort out the problematic of the lack of fit between local cultural and religious traditions, on the one hand, and human rights and the regime of international law, on the other. The existing standards of human rights can no doubt be enhanced by the input of different cultural traditions and values. However, one must remain ever alert to the possibility that even well-intentioned efforts to retool existing human rights standards, in order, for example, to eliminate features deemed excessively Western and to ground the standards on a new international consensus, may pose real dangers. The international standards of human rights are vital for the protection of human rights and should be left intact until new ones are found that promise to afford protections serving the goal of advancing human rights (and more generally, human well-being) at least as well as the ones now set forth in the International Bill of Human Rights. One important problem that we face is this: Without compromising the international framework of human rights, how are we to deal constructively with moral-cultural diversity?

An aspect of this problem that is particularly vexing is the practical issue of how to integrate human rights norms within differing cultural contexts so that these norms are genuinely absorbed into and shape both the moral psychology of persons and the moral ethos of communities. It is necessary to look for ways to supplement and enhance official standard-setting and implementation processes. In particular, there is the need to promote popular legitimacy for human rights norms not only in order to help generate the political will to enact and implement human rights standards, but also to achieve a sufficient level of voluntary compliance for enforcement to be effective. Since no system of enforcement can cope with massive and persistent violations of its normative standards, voluntary compliance must be the rule, rather than the exception. This compliance can only occur when human rights norms become an integral part of the moral psychology of persons and of the ethos of the community at large. It is therefore important to look for popular acceptance and support for human rights norms beyond official formulations, which means serious and sustained engagement with cultural moral traditions.[1] That is to say, we need to develop a strategy that is sensitive to both the goal of universality, on the one hand, and the reality of particular cultural traditions, on the other.

Part of the solution to this problem obviously involves holding governments accountable to the international law of human rights, but such accountability cannot be the whole answer. Some human rights principles—such as the prohibition of slavery, torture, and genocide—are peremptory norms, binding on all states regardless of whether they endorse them.[2] Some of the principles set forth in the Universal Declaration of Human Rights have by now been assimilated into customary international law, being thereby binding on states even if they have failed to ratify relevant treaties. However, some important human rights principles, from some viewpoints, may be binding only on states that have ratified the treaties in which they are set forth. Neither the instrumentality of treaties or of customary international law is completely satisfactory insofar as the universal validity and application of human rights are concerned. Both instrumentalities are premised on the agreement of sovereign states which, as the primary objects of limitation and accountability by human rights norms, are unlikely to be fully cooperative. Whereas customary international law is binding on all states, it tends to evolve very slowly, and its norms are difficult to ascertain and apply in specific cases. Treaties are binding only on states which have ratified them, can be limited by reservations even

---

[1] Our position here can be further elaborated in the following way. On the one hand, the concept and essential characteristics of current international human rights standards have been principally conceived, developed, and established within the cultural context of certain societies, primarily of Western Europe and North America. On the other hand, these standards cannot be accepted and implemented globally unless they are seen as valid from the perspectives of the peoples of other parts of the world. Otherwise, those peoples would have neither the desire to comply with nor the political will to enforce and implement international human rights standards. In other words, human rights efforts may be doomed to failure if they are seen to be premised on the universalization and implementation of a certain culturally specific (i.e., Western) model, rather than on the articulation and implementation of a genuinely universal model (e.g., achieved through dialogue and consensus by the peoples of the world).

[2] As it happens, no state or religious tradition is currently resisting these norms.

when ratified, and often require some form of state action for their implementation.

The problem is not universality per se, but rather *which* standards are universal and *how* these standards are formulated. Whoever has a universalized conception of human rights will not doubt be happy with universality, and so we must next consider the major players in the debate over universality vs. realtivism.

Speakers and their Perspectives

In order to understand properly the nature of human rights debates in general and the debate about universality vs. relativism in particular, it is essential to distinguish the perspectives of various classes of speakers or claimants. In the present debate we can distinguish three principal types of speakers: (i) state actors, (ii) NGOs, religious representatives, individual actors, and (iii) the oppressed, both individually and collectively. The last category often will be comprised of women. For each of these perspectives we need to ask critical questions about the speaker's position (e.g., powerful or powerless?), representation (e.g., on whose behalf?), motives (e.g., moral concern or self-interest?), language and collateral behavior (e.g., are actions consonant with discourse?), etc. Let us now consider each of the main perspectives in the debate.

State actors often represent themselves as speaking on behalf of an entire nation and sometimes an entire culture. They speak from a position of political power and often represent their motives as matters of concern for the welfare of a whole society or even a whole culture. Many state actors in the present debate use the language of cultural and moral relativism (versus universality of rights), ostensibly to defend the integrity of a way of life and/or a world view. Despite their claim of speaking representatively from moral motives, using the language of relativism to defend the integrity of a world view or way of life, the actions of many state actors belie the sincerity of their motives and their discourse, for it appears that such language is often used as a screen to perpetrate and to defend human rights violations for self-interested political ends. Since many of these actors do not have a representative democratic government, it is implausible that they are in a position to represent the views of an entire society, much less an entire culture. Since they often use force or the threat of force to quell dissent and to pursue internally repressive policies, it is implausible that they are acting from motives of genuine moral concern for the well-being of all citizens. There is considerable reason to be skeptical about appeals by undemocratic states to moral-cultural relativism or to the authority of a particular religious or cultural tradition, especially when these appeals are used to justify human rights abuses.[1] Where women's rights are concerned, states' credentials are especially suspect.

In our view, any claims by states that current international human rights standards must be adjusted to accommodate cultural differences need to be regarded with a high degree of skepticism. Spokespersons for undemocratic regimes are likely to speak on behalf of the political interests of the regimes that they represent, not on behalf of the cultures of the citizenry or the well-being of the citizenry. To date, governmental claims that culture justifies deviating from human rights standards have been made exclusively by states that have demonstrably bad human rights records. State invocations of "culture" and "cultural relativism" seem to be little more than cynical pretexts for rationalizing human rights abuses that particular states would in any case commit. If cultural pretexts for their violations of international human rights were not available, states now invoking cultural defenses would probably emulate China in appealing to the principle of national sovereignty in their efforts to delegitimize external criticism of their human rights records. Moreover, states such as Iran and Saudi Arabia, for example, maintain that they are following Islamic human rights norms, while failing to adhere even to the norms that they officially deem Islamic, indicating that the rights that they claim suit Islamic culture are no more respected than are other, supposedly Western rights.

Despite all that we have said here about the motives of state actors, it is nonetheless important to note that their political rhetorical strategies would not be used if they had no internal resonances within their respective societies. But we must also caution that such resonances themselves need to be subjected to critical scrutiny and analysis by asking such questions as: Do these strategies resonate with only selected groups, and how are these groups characterized? Do these strategies resonate with oppressed groups within the respective societies; and if they do not, then what bearing does this fact have on assessing the legitimacy of the rhetoric? For example, many states refuse to ratify the Convention on the Elimination of all Forms of Discrimination Against Women, which has been in force since 1981, claiming that their culture precludes such ratification. Or they may ratify the Convention but enter reservations on cultural grounds. Many men in the societies involved may approve of such state policies opposing equal rights for women, but the "cultural" justifications may seem less plausible to women in these same societies.

The cynical and self-serving invocations of cultural defenses for state oppression and denials of human rights must be clearly distinguished from the

---

[1] On this point, see, e.g., Ann Elizabeth Mayer, "Universal Versus Islamic Human Rights: A Clash of Cultures or a Clash with a Construct?" *Michigan Journal of International Law 15*, (1994, in press).

positions taken by NGOs and individuals genuinely concerned to accommodate human rights within differing cultural traditions. This latter class of speakers may use elements of local culture to reconceptualize human rights principles and formulations in ways that could potentially enhance respect for human rights. These speakers do not operate from a position of self-interested power, and they attempt to speak on behalf of the oppressed. They may try to translate human rights norms into cultural idioms so that these norms might be more effectively recognized and respected. It appears entirely justifiable to treat this discourse, as contrasted with that of state actors, as decently motivated and constructive.

The third class of speakers in the debate about universality vs. relativism in human rights is the most important one. Theirs are the voices of the oppressed whose human rights are being violated, and it is our belief that their suffering entitles them to be authentic witnesses about what oppression is like and how it works. Outsiders seeking to understand where different cultures and religious traditions stand on human rights questions need to be careful to take into account the voices of groups and individuals on the receiving end of governmental policies and to listen to the perspectives of oppressed members of societies where international human rights are being rejected and violated.[1] The voices of states on issues of human rights are louder than those of individuals or representatives of civil society, especially in countries where it is most urgent for the voices of the latter to register. And the voices of states are often particularly effective in deflecting attention away from the voices of the oppressed. The voices of women, most often the losers where culture is invoked to justify rights violations, are likely to be stifled. The high rates of female illiteracy in many countries are obstacles to communicating women's pespectives. Women therefore may need assistance in articulating their claims and in getting them to be heard. Fortunately, some of these voices have gained the ear of the world, and we must do all we can to amplify them.

The world cannot help but recognize the voices of moral authenticity (e.g., that of the Dalai Lama), and it is to be emphasized that *these voices have little or no difficulty with the notion of universal human rights norms.* We must not rely exclusively on governmental statements about what local culture requires and about the alleged incompatibility of such requirements with international human rights. That the oppressed have no difficulty with the universality of human

---

[1] We must, of course, be cautious not to impose our own assumptions about what the oppressed "really" want or "must" want. It must be understood that many oppressed voices are likely to reach us through NGOs and individual human rights advocates (i.e., the preceding group of speakers), rather than independently and directly; the Dalai Lama, for example, is just such an intermediary.

rights is a significant moral message that cannot go unheeded in the present debate.[1]

Cultural Complexity

It is rare for the boundaries of a modern nation-state to coincide with cultural boundaries. Nonetheless, governments that invoke cultural pretexts for denying rights tend to talk as if there were a unitary, monolithic culture that is shared by their citizens. A good example in this connection is the military dictatorship in Sudan, which invokes "Islam" to justify its deplorable human rights record and ignores the fact that the "fundamentalist" version of Islam that it imposes on its citizenry is not shared by most Sudanese Muslims. It also ignores the fact that its Islamization and Arabization policies have alienated one-third of the Sudanese population, which is neither Muslim nor Arab. Against such attempts to speak on behalf of totalized versions of cultures, it must be clearly recognized that every society and every culture is comprised of diverse views about significant issues of human life and human well-being, including, of course, issues of human rights. Some of these latter views embrace human rights as universally applicable standards and urge their enculturation as such. Other views do not embrace all recognized human rights standards as universal but instead see certain standards as contestable within the culture, thereby posing the problem of how to bridge the gaps between (a) these views and universalist positions internal to the society or culture, and (b) these views and universalist positions outside the society or culture.

One of the principal problems that stands in the way of diffusing a better understanding of human rights in non-Western societies is the gap that often prevails between two particular groups. One group tends to be relatively secular and universalist in its approach to human rights. To this group belong intellectuals and professionals familiar with international law and the major independent human rights groups and organizations. The other group consists of clerics and religious leaders familiar with their own cultural traditions but typically not well-versed in international law and human rights. Although the two groups may have more in common than they would suppose in terms of shared aspirations for more freedoms and rights, learning from each other is impeded by the gap in their respective discourses; one group is grounded in

---

[1] We also need to recognize that oppression can be so subtle and pervasive that the "oppressed" might not necessarily consider themselves oppressed; e.g., racist and sexist policies or other class divisions might not be obvious to all who are forced to live with their effects. Such deeply ingrained oppression could result in views which might obscure the appeal of universal human rights. We are indebted to Tracy Coleman (see opening acknowledgments) for reminding us of this point.

principles of international law and the other in moral and religious concepts. Persons equally grounded in both traditions are rare. Moreover, because women have been pervasively excluded from rising to positions of religious leadership, women's voices are rarely taken into account in the articulation of religious precepts, which may reflect strong male biases and lack of empathy for the cause of women's rights. Bridging this "discourse gap" could lead to fruitful cross-fertilization, and devising creative means to achieve this goal should be given priority.

Where there are efforts to bridge such gaps, thereby initiating nascent human rights dialogues internal to societies and cultures, state actors often try to interfere in two ways. First, as we have seen, they often claim unpersuasively that they represent cultures and are the principal arbiters of culture, a claim that not only illegitimately totalizes cultures but also is manifestly untrue when significant dissent is ignored or discounted. Second, state actors often use political power, including force, to quash dialogue, and, therefore, to forestall potential dissent to state policies which are inimicable to human rights. Such claims and interferences must be exposed and denounced if internal cultural dialogues are to have any effective future. It should not go unnoticed that an important lesson to be learned from all of this is that human rights strategists and advocates must themselves avoid the trap of totalizing cultures, not merely to avoid colluding with and giving aid and comfort to state actors in their totalizing rhetoric, but also, and more importantly, to continue fostering human rights dialogues internal to and between cultural traditions.

TOWARD A STRATEGY OF RESOLUTION

Despite the challenges posed by the universality vs. relativism debate, there is clear evidence that human rights and associated concepts of human dignity and equality have considerable moral appeal both within and across cultures. Such evidence ranges from the progress of nearly fifty years toward international recognition of human rights, to the work of human rights advocates in NGOs across the world and to human rights support within religious communities of diverse cultures. In the latter regard, many religious leaders and interfaith commissions during this century not only have articulated concepts and norms of human dignity and equality apparently acceptable to a wide range of traditions, but also have expressed firm support for human rights in the language of their own traditions, proclaiming that human rights are both international law and, more significantly, for example, "the law of God."[1] Even the "Global Ethic" of the 1993 Parliament of the World's Religions, signed by religious leaders from over twenty religious traditions, demonstrates the solidarity among many traditions, while avoiding the explicit language of human rights, in their mutual recognition of the priority of the subject-matter of many human rights.[2] Furthermore, views beginning to be articulated in a variety of religious traditions challenge teachings that deny equal rights to women.

We believe that such developments strongly suggest that the universality vs. relativism debate in human rights can be most effectively addressed by demonstrating how moral dialogue internal to and between religious and cultural traditions is not only possible, but also may lead to significant agreement on human rights norms and issues.[3] In what follows, we sketch some of the more important parameters for a dialogical response to, and possible resolution of, this debate. This strategy has a number of distinct elements, each of which warrants careful attention: (1) adoption of crucial moral premises, (2) self-criticism about past human rights advocacy, (3) affirmation of ongoing human rights dialogues and support for their expansion, and (4) the setting of an agenda for multi-level human rights dialogues.

CRUCIAL MORAL PREMISES

In supporting both intracultural and intercultural human rights dialogues, it is absolutely crucial to affirm existing standards of international human rights as a primary frame of reference. This is critical for a number of reasons. There is an undeniable legal consensus stemming from ratifications of various human rights conventions, as well as from customary international law. This legal consensus also forms the basis for a moral consensus, since human rights represent both moral and legal claims that individuals and groups can assert and that state and international actors are responsible for protecting. If we were to scrap this hard-won consensus, it might be difficult, given the political realities of our current

---

[1] For this point and its formulation, we are indebted to a private communication from Robert Traer (see opening acknowledgments), in response to the earlier draft of this paper.

[2] For the text of this "Global Ethic," as well as illuminating commentaries on the process of drafting and ratification, see Hans Küng and Karl-Josef Kuschel , edds., *A Global Ethic: The Declaration of the Parliament of the World's Religions* (New York: Continuum Publishing Co., 1993). See also Küng's earlier book, *Global Responsibility: In Search of a New World Ethic* (New York: Continuum Publishing Co., 1993).

[3] For some illuminating efforts at such dialogical approaches to human rights, see the articles in Abdullahi An-Na'im, ed., *Human Rights in Cross-Cultural Perspectives* (Philadelphia: University of Pennsylvania, 1992).

world, to get back to where we are. There is no point in either denying or rolling back moral and legal progress, even if some premises are, at least in part, contestable. Moreover, human rights standards appear crucial for acknowledging and protecting internal cultural-moral discourse. This last point warrants particular elaboration.

While we would concede that some human rights norms are contested within societies and cultures, it is undeniable that many norms are accepted as relatively uncontestable.[1] That is to say, there are some human rights set forth in international law that remain uncontested even by those calling for the recognition of cultural differences. These rights include freedom from torture, slavery, genocide, and racial discrimination; the requirements of fair trial; and respect for the dignity of the human person. Moreover, certain other human rights norms, even if contested, must be presupposed for any legitimate dialogue to take place. Since even the contesters must presuppose these norms for themselves, they appear rationally compelled, for the purposes of dialogue, to grant them, however provisionally, to their dialogical partners. Here we have in mind those human rights that may be contested by advocates of cultural relativist approaches to human rights, among them the rights to freedom of expression, freedom of the press, freedom of religion, and freedom of association. To allow the undermining of rights such as these would be to curb, if not eliminate, precisely the freedoms that are needed to carry out meaningful dialogue on human rights and to seriously impede the project of more firmly establishing cultural foundations for a global human rights system. Affirming these human rights norms, even while distinguishing uncontested from contested norms, comprises a fundamental floor of moral agreement that permits constructive dialogue to take place.

---

[1] As an illustration of the importance of drawing such a distinction between non-controversial and contestable human rights norms, consider the following. Although Islamic law has many principles and values that are relevant for formulating rights, in the past it has had no exact counterparts of modern rights, and it still has no human rights theory and precepts that Muslims regard as definitive. All of the positions on rights that purport to state Islamic principles have been articulated quite recently and vary greatly. Some of these positions diverge sharply from norms of international law, diverging most sharply regarding the rights of women, religious freedom, discrimination against religious minorities, and corporal punishment for crimes. These are areas where there is Quranic authority for interpretations that present obstacles, although not necessarily insuperable, to accepting human rights. In other areas, as where Muslims claim that Islam precludes democratic government, the claims are less firmly grounded in Islamic authority and more readily subject to challenge. On some rights, such as the prohibition of torture or the right to self-determination, Muslims do not claim to have a distinctive Islamic position at odds with international norms. One therefore needs to differentiate between those areas where there are potentially serious conflicts over settled interpretations of the Islamic sources and human rights principles and other areas where conflicts between Islamic law and international law are less acute or even nonexistent.

There is great diversity in non-Western perspectives on human rights, and the full range of perspectives deserves to be aired and considered. Open and free dialogues over such differences are bound to be beneficial for human rights. To have such discussions, protection for human rights advocacy is essential. This protection requires that governments be pressured to respect existing international human rights laws which protect freedom of expression and association. Governmental measures to thwart attempts to disseminate human rights ideas and to crush both independent human rights organizations and dialogues have stalled the reception of human rights norms in non-Western traditions. Such measures have also impeded chances for these traditions to evolve in ways that would enable them to make their own contributions to human rights.

A second type of premise crucially important to intracultural and intercultural human rights dialogues is the relevance of cultural, moral, religious, and philosophical factors in the dialogues. In the past there has been some reluctance to admit these factors as relevant to the articulation of any human rights norms.[1] This reluctance appears to have been fueled by the specious reasoning associated with what is known as the slippery slope (or alternatively, the camel's nose under the tent): If some human rights norms are adjusted in light of cultural moral values, then all rights will eventually go the same way, thereby threatening important moral and legal constraints on government behavior. This reasoning, of course, overlooks the consideration that when distinctions are reasonably drawn and affirmed, then the slope is no longer slippery (or what was thought to be a slope turns out to be a clearly fenced level field).

With regard to the debate over universality vs. relativism in human rights, it must be said that failure to admit the relevance of cultural factors would be extremely counter-productive. The point of encouraging dialogue about this issue is to examine critically the role of cultural factors and to make precise and informed judgments about the scope of their relevance. Obviously, this dialogue cannot take place if such factors are excluded *ab initio*. Moreover, inasmuch as one very important goal of such dialogue is to see human rights taken up by and become integral to the moral psychology and ethos of all societal contexts and cultural traditions, then it appears that these factors must perforce be taken seriously. Worries about the potential effects of scrapping the hard-won standards of international human rights are clearly countervailed by the affirmation of existing standards as a primary frame of reference for such dialogue, as discussed above. In fact, the willingness to admit the relevance of cultural factors signals not the rolling back of moral and legal progress in human

---

[1] On this point, see, e.g., Alston, "Human Rights in 1993" and An-Na'im, *Human Rights in Cross-Cultural Perspectives*, especially An-Na'im's own contributions to this volume.

rights but rather a coming of age or an appropriate maturity about their complexity *vis-a-vis* cultural contexts.[1]

Needless to say, any genuine human rights dialogue about contestable norms and issues must presuppose a foundational commitment to open-mindedness and a willingness to be changed by reasoned and persuasive argument from other points of view. Such commitment is crucial to giving equal respect to all dialogical partners, and it appears to entail being aware of and being willing to suspend power disparities among them, for moral truth is not correlated with political power. Especially important in this regard is the self-conscious effort to empower, listen to, and heed the morally authentic voices of the oppressed in any dialogue about human rights.

SELF-CRITICISM

Self-criticism about past handling of human rights norms and issues is important for gaining the serious attention and participation of cultural traditions in human rights dialogues, for it displays in a concrete way the good faith of participants in being open-minded and willing to change through a mutually critical dialogue in which all are regarded and treated as equals. Self-criticism is required at a number of levels, including, for example, foreign policy, domestic policy, and nongovernmental individual and group discourse and action.

Critique of foreign policy, for example, might appropriately focus on state actors' use of a double-standard with regard to respecting and protecting human rights throughout the world. This level of self-criticism seems especially applicable to the foreign policy of Western nations. Since Western societies are closely associated with the existing regime of international human rights, consistent and even-handed human rights policies on the part of the West promote the cause of human rights. In contrast, biased and selective protest over human rights violations in non-Western societies undermines the credibility of international human rights. Of course, unevenness and bias on the part of Western governments in efforts to protect human rights will have even wider negative repercussions. Thus, for example, the lack of even-handedness embodied in the West's long neglect of the suffering of the Palestinians and the indifference it has shown to the plight of Bosnian Muslims are precisely what need rethinking in order to disarm critics who charge that human rights are

---

[1] On this point, see Alston, "Human Rights in 1993."

merely tools of Western imperialism, rather than principles applicable to non-Western, as well as to Western, peoples.[1]

Critique of internal domestic policies that bear on human rights range from egregious cases of torture, systematic rape, and "disappearances," to mistreatment of indigenous peoples, the dispossessed, and homeless people, and to various forms of discrimination (e.g., on the basis of gender, race, ethnic background, religious affiliation). This level of self-criticism is no less applicable to Western societies than it is to non-Western societies. It seems plausible to contend that Western nations fail to live up to a number of human rights standards and to apply these standards consistently to their internal social structures and practices. There are, for example, significant human rights violations here in the United States: consider the level and extent of poverty within a nation that has one of the highest standards of living in the world; consider too the health care inequities among social and economic classes, the continuing problems of gender and racial discrimination, the treatment of homeless people (a dispossessed population, surely), and the treatment of Native American peoples. Such cases clearly indicate, once again, the employment of a double standard in the West's criticism of the domestic policies of other societies and its simultaneous blindness to its own human rights violations. Critical self-reflection, then, is called for by Westerners who tend to be excessively smug in their assumptions about the impeccability of Western human rights records. In fact, Western rights records often leave much to be desired, something that should be frankly acknowledged. Efforts to use culture and religion to advance human rights should not be seen as a project by the West to raise societies elsewhere to the West's unimpeachable standards. Instead, Westerners should view themselves as being in partnership with members of non-Western cultures in a common project to establish a truly global human rights culture.

Critique of nongovernmental individuals and groups also seems appropriate to self-criticism about regard for human rights. Here we are thinking especially

---

[1] U.S. foreign policy has been associated with efforts to promote human rights since the Carter era, and to a large extent the United States represents the West. The ideals of human rights have enormous resonance in, e.g., the Muslim world. By launching a policy in the 1970s of securing respect for human rights, the United States awakened great expectations. Had the United States promoted human rights in a consistent and even-handed manner, the credibility of international human rights may have increased. Instead, selective and opportunistic practices in applying human rights to foreign policy issues left the impression that human rights were for Christians and Jews, not for Muslims. Western indifference to the plight of the Palestinians, the sufferings of the Iranians under the Shah, and the harsh impact of the post-Gulf War sanctions on the Iraqi population were taken as proof of bias and selectivity in the application of human rights. Above all, the failure of the West to definitively come to the rescue of Bosnia has embittered Muslims and convinced many that appeals to human rights are a sham.

of those voices expressing views that appear to collude with the problematic foreign and domestic policies of state actors. Consider, for example, the dehumanization associated with "Orientalism" and other forms of ethnocentricity and cultural stereotyping (e.g., the still- pervasive stereotype of so-called "primitive" and "uncivilized" tribal peoples); the ideological blindness of those cultural critics who value civil and political rights to the virtual exclusion of social and economic rights; and the "fanaticism" of those religious leaders who would deny the dignity and equality of persons and groups on the basis of sexual orientation, ethnic identity, and birth status; and the list could continue.

The fact that such biased attitudes can have very deleterious effects may be illustrated by the following example. Influenced by "Orientalist" stereotypical attitudes toward Islam, people in the West have tended to perceive Islam as a monolith, a perspective reinforced by Muslims who purvey an ideologized version of Islam. Both groups see Islam as a self-contained culture opposed to the West and as precluding the reception of human rights, which are viewed as distinctively Western. Empirical verification is rarely attempted, so many people in the West miss the actual diversity of opinion among Muslims on human rights issues. That there could be genuine dissidents in Islam does not seem to occur to many Westerners, who tend to accord far too much weight to governmental representations about what Islam requires. Westerners' ability to perceive that there are Muslims who live out their commitment to international human rights is further impeded by censorship and distortions. Where they encounter Muslims who advocate the universality of human rights, many Westerners tend to treat them as persons necessarily alienated from their own tradition. Unfortunately, this perspective corresponds to the very position taken by the "fundamentalist" and conservative Muslims opposed to human rights. These people accuse Muslims who advocate the universality of human rights of being Westernized secularists who are disentitled to speak about Islam. The unholy alliance is made possible by dehumanizing ethnocentrism.[1]

---

[1] Here it might be appropriate to enter a note about the role of the press. Clearly, the educational potential of the press could be invaluable as a way to counter and help dissolve stereotypical assumptions. Unfortunately, the public (e.g., in the United States) knows little about other countries and cultures, and the press often does little to educate its readers in an unbiased and complete way. In our view, the press could do a better job in educating the public so that cultural stereotypes would have less chance of deleteriously affecting people's views and the social ethos. Again, we are indebted to Tracy Coleman (see opening acknowledgments) for suggesting this point. For an illuminating diagnosis and critique of how the U.S. press has affected public views of China, e.g., see Henry Rosemont, Jr., *A Chinese Mirror: Moral Reflections on Political Economy and Society* (La Salle, IL: Open Court, 1991).

We believe that self-criticism at these three levels by all participants in human rights dialogues would have a number of salutary effects, not least of which would be the conferral of credibilty upon one's own discourse; the collapsing, or at least mitigation, of the distinction between "outsider" and "insider" regarding human rights criticism (in some respects, all groups and traditions are human rights "sinners"); the promotion of consistency in the application of human rights standards; and, of course, the promotion of a global human rights culture. And we would emphasize that listening to what the victims of human rights abuses have to say would serve as an important guide to the places where self-criticism is needed. To paraphrase what Albert Camus' fictional character Tarrou rightly says in *The Plague*, in cases of ambiguity and indecision, always ask who is the victim and then take the victim's side. If we follow this advice, we cannot go far wrong.

SUPPORTING ONGOING HUMAN RIGHTS DIALOGUES

There are a number of ongoing human rights dialogues that form the initial basis for multi-level global discussion of universality vs. relativism. Examples of such dialogues range from various interfaith commissions to the activity of NGOs at the 1993 human rights conference in Vienna.[1] Although excluded from the process of drafting the final conference declaration, these NGOs nonetheless joined forces to denounce the exploitation of cultural relativism as a pretext for human rights violations, especially regarding the systematic oppression of women throughout the world. Such efforts provide evidence for the possibility and fruitfulness of further developing a coordinated dialogical human rights strategy at two levels: (a) internal cultural dialogues, in which the diversity of moral views within traditions are clearly acknowledged and engaged; and (b) cross-cultural dialogues, in which different traditions can become aware of their commonalities and debate their differing perspectives on contestable human rights norms and issues.

It is our considered judgment that such multi-level dialogues have the best chance of resolving or at least reducing conflict over human rights norms. They would do this in a variety of ways. First, such dialogues are likely to strengthen intercultural recognition of, and compliance with, core human rights norms, putting moral pressure on societies and cultures that are recalcitrant. Second,

---

[1] For an overview of interfaith activities and declarations, see Marcus Braybrooke, *Stepping Stones to a Global Ethic* (London: SCM Press Ltd., 1992). For discussion of NGO activity at the 1993 Vienna conference, see Mayer, "Universal Versus Islamic Human Rights," especially section III. B.

such dialogues are likely to assist human rights initiatives, debates, and reforms within cultural traditions, encouraging and supporting the process of hearing and taking seriously diverse voices, especially those of oppressed classes and groups. Third, such dialogues are likely to encourage the sustained development of a moral psychology and ethos oriented toward human rights in the world's communities and traditions. Finally, as they spread and advance, such dialogues are likely to pressure state actors to conform with human rights standards by holding them increasingly accountable for conventions they have ratified, as well as for maintaining standards of customary international law.

AGENDA OF ISSUES

As a practical step toward encouraging the extension of these multi-level human rights dialogues, we believe it important to identify certain contestable human rights norms and issues that appear to be particularly representative of the universality vs. relativism debate, as well as being of particular concern to moral and religious traditions. These norms and issues involve cultural, moral, and religious values apparently in particular tension with the universality of human rights. By identifying these norms and issues and proposing how they might be discussed constructively, we aim to raise awareness of seemingly intractable issues, to provide hope for the possibility of resolution, and to suggest the importance of dialogical strategies.

The representative issues that must be addressed, and this list is not meant to be exhaustive, include: (a) survival rights pertaining to the provision of adequate levels of food and other essential needs, inasmuch as, e.g., these rights may be negatively affected by beliefs and values favoring spiritual over material needs; (b) gender equality and the status of women, with special attention to women's control over their bodily integrity (including sexuality) and marital and reproductive choices, and the social and economic discrimination women encounter; (c) freedom of religious belief and problems of social and economic discrimination on the basis of religious identity; (d) caste and birth status and problems of social and economic discrimination based on such status; (e) discrimination against indigenous peoples and ethnic groups; and (f) discrimination on religious grounds against other groups, e.g., gays or AIDS sufferers. In addition, the following background issues deserve consideration: (i) the status of moral and cultural relativism within philosophical and religious traditions; (ii) alternative moral and philosophical bases for justifying and articulating human rights standards; and (iii) what are thought to be distinctively new human rights and associated standards and procedures—e.g., ecologically oriented rights, cultural rights, rights to development, and consensual and conciliatory (vs. legal adversarial) adjudication procedures. In one way or another, all of these issues involve significant interaction with religious beliefs and practices.[1]

With respect to each of these issues, we recommend the following procedure for examination and assessment: (a) show exactly how and why there is a tension among cultural, moral, and religious values, on the one hand, and human rights standards as currently construed, on the other; (b) examine the bases for internal traditional values and try to determine how closely they are tied to the premises of the traditions (consider, e.g., whether they are perhaps more a consequence of socio-economic factors); (c) explore the question of whether the traditions themselves incorporate diverse interpretations of these values, as well as the sources of justification for such values; (d) place this internal diversity of views in dialogue with other cultural and religious traditions and with the international human rights community in order to (i) identify commonalities as well as divergences in moral content and justification of human rights, and (ii) identify and draw out analogies that may facilitate expansions and convergences of the human rights subject matter at issue; and finally, (e) recommend a critical resolution of the issue, establishing a spectrum of standards and indicating the limits of tolerable diversity, while encouraging movement to higher standards of attainment.

In order to validate, if only partially and somewhat superficially, the utility of our recommended procedure for the dialogical examination of human rights issues, we used it to achieve consensus within our own group in preparing this paper. Although we do not have the space to recount this process point by point, we can report that we successfully moved from a tension between a more philosophically-oriented contextual position and a more legalistically-oriented universalist position—represented by a majority report and an impending minority report—to a position that is culturally sensitive and yet advocates the

---

[1] For a preliminary discussion of some of these issues, see Robert Traer, *Faith in Human Rights* (Washington, D. C.: Georgetown University Press, 1991). For the perceptive identification of issue (i), we are indebted to Alston, "Human Rights in 1993." Other relevant preliminary discussions of some of these issues includes, e.g., Randle Edwards, Louis Henkin, and Andrew Nathan, eds., *Human Rights in Contemporary China* (New York: Columbia University Press, 1986); Alfred T. Hennelly and John Langan, eds., *Human Rights in the Americas* (Washington, D. C.: Georgetown University Press, 1982); David Little, John Kelsay, and A. Sachedina, *Human Rights and the Conflict of Cultures: Western and Islamic Perspectives on Religious Liberty* (Columbia, SC: University of South Carolina Press, 1988); Ann Elizabeth Mayer, *Islam and Human Rights: Tradition and Politics* (Boulder: Westview Press, 1991); Leroy Rouner, ed., *Human Rights and the World's Religions* (South Bend: Princeton of Notre Dame Press, 1988). See also works cited in the footnotes above and below.

universality of human rights as a normative goal. Creative moral dialogue does work if the parties can be self-critical, open-minded, responsive to reasoned argument from alternative perspectives, and ever sensitive to the fact that the most important consideration in any moral discussion is heeding the voices of the oppressed.

TWO ILLUSTRATIONS OF URGENT ISSUES

Of the various issue-areas that we have identified for future intracultural and intercultural dialogue, two appear particularly urgent, if only because they have been largely ignored until very recently: (a) gender discrimination and mistreatment on purported cultural and religious grounds; and (b) discrimination and mistreatment of indigenous peoples on grounds that they are "other" than the dominant majority culture and an unwelcome reminder, strategically and emotionally, that they were wrongfully displaced from their ancestral lands. If, as a world community, we could solve these problems in part through internal and cross-cultural moral dialogue, then we would be that much closer to resolving many of the other issues. It would be unwarrantly presumptuous for our small consultation group to apply in any definitive way our recommended procedure to these issues; it is, after all, designed as a dialogical strategy to be employed by representatives of cultural traditions. Nonetheless, it may be instructive at least to limn how the procedure might be used to approach these issues.

Women's Human Rights: The Case of FGM

Female genital mutilation (FGM) is a vivid example of how women can be deleteriously affected by an oppressive social practice that is reinforced, if not sustained, by patriarchically infused cultural and religious values. It is estimated that as many as 90-100 million women in Africa and the Middle East have been subjected to this ritual practice, which carries serious, documented medical and psychological complications ranging from hemorrhaging, chronic infections, and HIV transmission to long-term emotional and developmental trauma.[1] The

---

[1] This estimate is reported by Evelyn C. White, "Alice Walker's Compassionate Crusade," *Sojourner: The Women's Forum* (March 1994), p. 1h. Although White extends the range of this practice into Asia as well, it is not clear that FGM occurs there. The practice occurs predominantly in Africa, although it may cross over into the Arabian penninsula and, more tenuously, be associated with the Middle East.

infliction of such a practice upon women raises a set of human rights issues. [1] Is this practice a consequence of cultural and religious discrimination against women as an oppressed class? To what extent is it possible to distinguish religious and cultural factors from socio-economic and political factors? Is there evidence indicating hope for a humane resolution of this issue?

Following our recommended procedure, we would need first to show exactly how and why there is a tension between cultural and religious values, on the one hand, and human rights standards, on the other. In the context of Sudan, for example, Nahid Toubia reports that the practice of FGM is often described as having the strength of a religious belief or ritual and is in tension with the human right of respect for personal bodily integrity.[2] She further argues that the practice is bound to an ideological subjugation of women that is reinforced by the Islamic tradition's suspicion of women's sexuality. Thus, this practice appears on its face to cause a severe tension between human rights and cultural-religious values.

Yet, to press the second question and next step of our designated procedure, what exactly are the bases for these religious values, and how closely are they tied to the premises of the traditions in question? Toubia proposes three considerations bearing on this question. First, she regards the practice of FGM as a ritual "inherited from an untraceable past that has no rational meaning and lies within the realm of the untouchable sensitivity of traditonal people." Second, the deepest past of this traditional social and cultural context was that of a matrilineal family system in which women had a positive and powerful social role, which was changed through "a process of capital concentration and surplus accumulation" to a form of patriarchy that has projected and treated women as "natural, wild, and uncontrollable." Third, although Islamic thought and practice may incorporate, in some of its versions, a complementary patriarchal view of

---

[1] Much of this mutilation is coerced and generally inflicted on very young girls who have no choice in an operation that has lifelong repercussions. In our view, such a practice obviously violates a woman's bodily integrity and therefore her human right to physical integrity.

[2] Nahid F. Toubia, "The Social and Political Implications of Female Circumcision: The Case of the Sudan," in Elizabeth Warnock Fernea , ed., *Women and the Family in the Middle East: New Voices of Change* (Austin: University of Texas Press, 1985), pp. 148-59. Toubia actually characterizes the practice as "a form of social injustice" (which it is as well), but violation of the human right of personal integrity is the specific violation that this injustice constitutes. Since the time that Toubia wrote her article, "female circumcision" has been replaced by the more vivid and accurate term "female genital mutilation."

women's potentially dangerous and destructive sexuality, this tradition does not itself endorse drastic forms of FGM.[1]

This analysis strongly suggests that the practice of FGM may not be an entailment of deeply held religious beliefs at all, but rather more a consequence of colonialist-influenced socio-economic factors operating under the guise of supposed traditional religious values. Moreover, this analysis clearly opens up a space for critical dialogue about the internal cultural legitimacy of such a practice and about whether it is not itself in serious tension with the deepest religious and moral beliefs of the relevant traditions: e.g., a positive valuation of women's social power and role in traditional African society and culture, as well as a more postive valuation of women within Islamic thought, which, even if it falls short of recognizing gender equality, nonetheless would be generally repulsed by a practice of systematic mutilation. Furthermore, it would be disingenuous to suggest that these traditions cannot be changed to incorporate even greater respect for women as the moral and legal equals of men.[2] What gives the lie to this possible contention is the recognition of considerable moral diversity within the Islamic tradition and the recognition that many Africans are becoming increasingly aware of the moral values imbedded in their traditions and of the way that these values may have been submerged, warped, or derailed by the socio-economic consequences of colonialism. There are, then, grounds for thinking that a dialogical strategy could help resolve this problem in favor of advancing women's human rights by dismantling the practice of FGM.

Furthermore, the recent history of polarization and rapprochement over Western and non-Western perceptions of FGM illustrates how reactions to cultural differences can lead to political clashes that impede the resolution of a human rights problem and also how misunderstandings on these points can be cleared up. Until recently, there were pervasive tensions between Western critics of FGM and spokespersons for African societies where FGM was common. Contributing to these tensions was a sense that Western critics of FGM were condemning the cultures involved as primitive and were passing arrogant

---

[1] Toubia, "The Social and Political Implications of Female Circumcision," pp. 150-51; quotations from p. 150. It should be mentioned here that there is some authority in Islamic law for permitting "minor" clipping.

[2] For an extensive discussion of this point, see Ann Elizabeth Mayer, "Cultural Particularism as a Bar to Women's Rights: Reflections on the Middle Eastern Experience," in Julie Peters and Andrea Wolper, eds., *Women and Human Rights: An Agenda for Change* (New York: Routledge, 1994, forthcoming), and the more focused discussion of the FGM issue in [Student author], NOTE: "What's Culture Got to do with It? Exercising the Harmful Tradition of Female Circumcision" 106 *Harvard Law Review* 1944, 1993. See also Abdullahi An-Na'im, *Toward an Islamic Reformation: Civil Liberties, Human Rights and International Law* (Syracuse: Syracuse University Press, 1990).

judgment on a practice that, in its cultural context, had meanings and functions other than those that Westerners assigned to it. Behind the resentment of Western criticisms was the impression that Westerners were talking down to members of the societies practicing FGM and resuscitating attitudes reminiscent of the era of Western colonialism, when the "White Man's Burden" was thought to be uplifting lesser breeds and civilizing the savages by rooting out practices that offended Western norms—FGM being taken as a perfect example. Defensive reactions and charges of cultural insensitivity were often provoked.

Partly as a result of improved communications between women's groups around the world, perceptions of the critiques of the practice of FGM have changed in the last few years. No longer do so many Africans see such critiques as emanating from insensitive, neo-colonialist attitudes. No longer is there such a wide gulf separating Western and African perceptions of the merits and harms of FGM. Increasingly, women in the West and in Africa who are struggling on behalf of women's rights have come to the realization that they share common experiences of oppression and that cross-cultural solidarities should be forged to combat all practices that harm women, whether they occur in the West or elsewhere. [1] This recognition has led to a shared, critical assessment of FGM and a disinclination to accept cultural and/or religious justifications for this practice. The way that the practice serves the patriarchal order and controls women's sexuality has been brought into sharp focus. Essential to the improved cross-cultural understanding has been the appreciation that women's rights advocates are not condemning African practices out of a conviction of Western cultural superiority, but they are offering consistent critiques of laws and customs that violate the human rights of women around the globe, in the West as well as in non-Western cultures.

Human Rights and Indigenous Peoples: Group Rights

One of the major tensions between, on the one hand, the cultural, moral, and religious values of indigenous peoples and, on the other, human rights standards concerns the status of group rights. The regime of human rights tends to focus on the importance of individual rights, while the cultural attitudes of indigenous peoples are largely focused on the importance of the group and its internal social relations (e.g., family, clan, community, and nation).[2] In the former case the

---

[1] Again, Mayer's work is useful here. See her "Cultural Particularism" article, cited above.

[2] This point is made by James W. Zion, "North American Indian Perspectives on Human Rights," in Abdullahi An-Na'im, ed., *Human Rights in Cross-Cultural Perspectives: A Quest for Consensus* (Philadelphia: University of Pennsylvania Press, 1992), pp. 191-220;

individual is clearly viewed as a social being but nonetheless can be legitimately perceived apart from the social context and, indeed, can be protected from the oppressive influence of that context. In the latter case, the individual cannot be so easily separated from the group, for it is only within the context of group relations that the individual has a real identity.[1] As a consequence of this difference in focus, indigenous peoples tend to interpret human rights concepts which are limited to the dignity and equality of individuals as principally assimilationist in goal and effect vis-a-vis their populations. The corollary is that thoroughgoing assimiliation means the destruction of the group, a type of ethnocide or genocide of a people's historical and cultural heritage and identity.[2]

The basis for indigenous peoples' orientation to internal group values is not adventitious, but rather represents a deep metaphysical and moral commitment to solidarity "reflected in the idea that dignity is achieved by fulfillment of understood roles, through community sharing, and by espousal of group rights as paramount over individual aspirations." [3] And it follows from this commitment that indigenous peoples believe that their communities have the right to determine their own destiny, government, and modes of advancing human dignity, determining which may overlap with international human rights in some respects but possibly deviate in others. Thus, on the face of the issue, there appears to be a significant tension or conflict between human rights and the cultural attitudes of indigenous peoples.

In order to advance beyond this conflict, or at least to reduce the tension, we suggest that future dialogue must wrestle with a number of issues encapsulated in the following questions: Is it true that the regime of human rights is, or needs to be, antipathetic to the notion of group or communal rights (e.g., the right of a people to determine the directions of its own society and culture)? Is it true that the attitudes of indigenous peoples are, or need to be, antipathetic to the notion of individual rights, and might these attitudes possibly incorporate a diversity of views on the relative importance of group versus individual rights? While we cannot here answer these questions in any definitive way, we can make a number of suggestions which, taken together, may indicate that this tension is far from being irresolvable.

---

see especially pp. 194-95. Zion is identified as General Counsel for the Navajo Housing Authority, a public agency of the Navajo Nation.

[1] See Zion, "North American Indian Perspectives," p. 203.

[2] Zion, "North American Indian Perspectives," p. 193.

[3] Allan McChesney, "Aboriginal Communities, Aboriginal Rights, and the Human Rights System in Canada," in An-Na'im, *Human Rights,* pp. 221-52; quotation from p. 222. McChesney is identified as being on the Faculty of Law of the University of Ottawa and was formerly Executive Director of the Legal Services Board (Legal Aid) of the Northwest Territories in Canada.

It is a misunderstanding that human rights exclude the recognition of group rights, for both of the international human rights Covenants acknowledge that "all peoples have the right to self-determination" (Article 1 of both Covenents). Although it may be true that there is no procedure for effectively arbitrating claims about the violation of this right, especially in cases of non-state entitites such as indigenous peoples, the acknowledgement concerning self-determination clearly shows that human rights thinking is not philosophically opposed to the concept of group or communal rights.[1] From the side of indigenous peoples, by the same token, claims that they are univerally opposed to recognizing rights other than communal rights are misrepresentations. While it is true that many of these peoples, individually or collectively, do not pursue avenues for redress of rights abuses through human rights commissions and other human rights instrumentalities, there is evidence to suggest that this choice is due less to firm philosophical objection to human rights per se than to a sense that such organs, procedures, and mechanisms are not particularly effective and are largely insensitive to the needs of indigenous peoples; further, there may be a perception that using human rights mechanisms may do more harm than good in the long run.[2] Indeed, in the case of at least some indigenous peoples—e.g., the Iroquois or Six Nations Confederacy—there is considerable evidence to suggest that individual human rights can co-exist with communal rights.[3] In the case of the Iroquois, the co-existence appears to be longstanding. In the 17th and 18th centuries, as well as in earlier centuries, according to Donald Grinde, "The fundamental laws of the Iroquois Confederacy espoused peace and brotherhood, unity, balance of power, the natural rights of all people, impeachment and removal, and the sharing of resources," and, "since the Iroquois were not inclined to give much power to authorities, unity, peace, and brotherhood were balanced against the natural rights of all people and the necessity of sharing resources equitably."[4] Oren Lyons, historian and contemporary spokesperson for

---

[1] This point is made by Paul Reeves, "Indigenous People and Human Rights," 19-page typescript of a paper delivered at Pennsylvania State University, October 13, 1993; see especially p. 5. We are indebted to Bishop Reeves, himself a Maori from New Zealand, for making his paper available to us.

[2] McChesney, "Aboriginal Communities," pp. 224-227. McChesney goes into considerable detail on this point, in addition to suggesting practical solutions; for the latter, see pp. 228-233.

[3] This point was forcefully articulated by Tonya Frichner, a member of the Onondaga Nation and President, American Indian Law Alliance, and Ingrid Washinawatok, a member of the Menominee Nation, in a recent meeting with the editors of this volume. The Confederacy includes the following peoples: the Onondaga, the Mohawk, the Seneca, the Cayuga, the Oneida, and the Tuscarora.

[4] Donald A. Grinde, Jr., "Iroquois Political Theory and the Roots of American Democracy," in Oren Lyons et al., *Exiled in the Land of the Free: Democracy, Indian Nations, and the U. S. Constitution* (Santa Fe: Clear Light Publishers, 1992), pp. 227-80

the Iroquois Confederacy, agrees, claiming that as early as 1000 A. D. "articulated in these traditions were inherent rights of the individual and the process with which to protect and exercise these rights."[1] Moreover, as with other cultural and religious traditions, we need to be alert to the fact that there is a diversity of views within indigenous groups; they too have their dissidents, minority interests, and feminists, who, while recognizing the importance of social and group rights, also may have a deep concern to argue that indigenous cultural attitudes must incorporate other human rights ideals and standards.[2]

Special sensitivity to group rights, however, seems to be called for in the case of indigenous peoples. They are uniquely vulnerable because they are not organized into states and therefore are underrepresented in international forums. Their traditional cultures also are often also uniquely fragile, being connected to natural environments over which they actually exercise little ultimate control and being surrounded by modern societies that tend to encroach on them.[3] To preserve their cultures and identities, they need zealously to protect their rights as a group. However, in so doing, they may infringe on what the modern world calls human rights. For example, the social organization of some indigenous peoples may follow rigid patriarchal models, in which women are subjugated to male authority and denied many rights. Insistence that such peoples observe international standards on women's rights could lead to the destruction of their already shaky social structure, harming their collective rights. In general, intact

---

(notes, pp. 378-94); quotes from pp. 238 and 241, respectively. Grinde argues, with considerable justification, that "the liberal ideas of the 17th and 18th century European philosophers [e.g., Locke and Rousseau] were a partial reflection of Native American [specifically, Iroquois] democratic principles" (p. 235). Another quote seems apt as well: "The ideal Iroquois personality exhibited tribal loyalty tempered with intellectual independence and autonomy. Iroquois people were trained to enter a society that was egalitarian, with power more equally distributed between male and female, young and old than in Euro-American society" (p. 236).

[1] Oren Lyons, with the resources of the American Indian Law Alliance, *What They Never Told Us* (New York: American Indian Law Alliance, 1993), p. 2. Lyons is Faithkeeper of the Turtle Clan, Onondaga Nation, and Professor of American Studies at SUNY, Buffalo. In a transcript of an oral interview with John Mohawk, member of the Seneca Nation and Lecturer in American Studies at SUNY, Buffalo, the interviewer, Kusumita P. Pedersen, asks a question about whether there is an American Indian equivalent to rights of the individual. Mohawk replies, "Absolutely.... I think especially [of] the Iroquois...what they call 'The Great Law.'" We are indebted to Pedersen and Mohawk for making this transcript available to us.

[2] On minority interests and human rights with respect to the indigenous peoples of Canada, see McChesney, "Aboriginal Communities," p. 242.

[3] Indeed, Howard Berman, professor at California Western School of Law, has observed that "Even if all the rights described in the recognized international instruments were implemented tomorrow, it would not be enough to ensure the survival of indigenous peoples as distinct peoples" (Conference on Religion and Human Rights, New York City, May 22-24, 1994).

traditional cultural systems of indigenous peoples should be left alone. Although officials of the national legal system of the surrounding modern society might prefer to refrain from interfering in a Fourth World culture within their own national borders, they might be drawn into a controversy against their will. A woman from an indigenous cultural group, for example, may call for modern courts to intercede to vindicate rights that she enjoys under national law or under the human rights treaties that the country has signed.[1] It may be that the woman plaintiff has a strong human rights claim, but that this claim is incompatible with the values of the collectivity to which she belongs. How to balance in such cases the claims of the individual vis-a-vis those of the collectivity, when both sides belong to vulnerable groups, presents agonizing dilemmas to which no thoughtful person would claim there are easy answers. Internal cultural dialogues as well as cross-cultural dialogues, conducted with a view to minimizing the harm to the indigenous culture and to individual claimants might help in reconciling respect for indigenous culture with the rights of the individual. It might also be observed here that the United Nations Draft Declaration on the Rights of Indigenous Peoples, while clearly emphasizing in the prologue "the fundamental importance of the right of self-determination of all peoples...[to] freely determine their political status and freely pursue their economic, social and cultural development," also explicitly says, for example, that "indigenous peoples have the right to the full and effective enjoyment of all human rights and fundamental freedoms" [in the International Bill of Human Rights] (Article 1); that "they have the individual rights to life, physical and mental integrity, liberty and security of person" (Article 6); that "particular attention shall be paid to the rights and special needs of indigenous elders, women, youth, children, and disabled persons" (Article 22); and that "all the rights and freedoms recognized herein are equally guaranteed to male and female indigenous individuals" (Article 43).[2] Thus, there is reason to expect that indigenous peoples embracing

---

[1] One such case, that of Sandra Lovelace in Canada, is discussed by Zion, "North American Indian Perspectives," pp. 192-93.

[2] The text of this draft declaration is reprinted as Appendix B in Alexander Ewen, ed., *Voice of Indigenous Peoples: Native People Address the United Nations* (Santa Fe: Clear Light Publishers, 1994), pp. 159-74. We are indebted to Clear Light Publishers for supplying us with free copies of its publications, *Exiled in the Land of the Free* (cited above) and *Voice of Indigenous Peoples*.

The Draft United Nations Declaration on the Rights of Indigenous Peoples (UN Doc. E/CN.4/Sub.2/1994/2/Add.1) was adopted by the Sub-Commission on Prevention of Discrimination and Protection of Minorities on August 26, 1994, and will be submitted to the Commission on Human Rights in 1995 for further action. The Sub-Commission is an expert body within the U.N. human rights system. The Draft Declaration was developed by a Sub-Commission working group in annual sessions between 1982 and 1993, with the participation of indigenous representatives and a number of observer governments.

this Draft Declaration will themselves develop mechanisms, if they do not have them already, to counteract untoward effects of patriarchy.

CONCLUSION

These two examples of women's and indigenous peoples' human rights demonstrate not only the utility of our recommended dialogical strategy for addressing the universality vs. relativism debate, but also the ever-present need to unmask the deep sources of apparent tensions between human rights and cultural particularity. We do not claim that this strategy will definitively resolve all such disputes, but we do claim that it has the long-range potential to mitigate them significantly and to encourage a moral psychology and ethos oriented toward human rights. Given the complexity of human societies, cultures, and religious traditions, it is probable that at least some tensions will remain and that new tensions will emerge. The key, of course, is maintaining the evolution of universal human rights as legitimate and relevant to people's lives in all parts of the world. We believe that a dialogical strategy has the best chance of ensuring such a result.

This paper of the Project on Religion and Human Rights has gone through several stages of preparation. The final draft has been prepared by Harvey Cox and Arvind Sharma, co-chairs of the Consultation Group on Positive Resources of Religion for Human Rights. During the process of its evolution, drafts were prepared in consultation with Preston Williams, Margaret Guider, Susannah Heschel, Robert Traer, and Talat Sait Halman. Help in its preparation from the following members of the Project on Religion and Human Rights is gratefully acknowledged: Paul Moore, Jr., Rabbi J. Rolando Matalon, Kusumita Pedersen, John Kelsay, David Little, Charles Strozier, Abdullahi An-Na'im, Sumner Twiss, William Wipfler, and Stanley Tambiah.

4

Positive Resources of Religion for Human Rights

The popular media are full of ugly reports and images of violence and human rights violations that are said to be inspired by religion. Angry Hindus tear down a Muslim mosque on December 6, 1991. At regular intervals pictures of the saddened relatives of yet another victim of the bloodshed among Christians in Northern Ireland fill the front pages. Muslim militants demand the death of a woman writer in Bangladesh. Muslim women are raped, as a systematic weapon of terrorism, by soldiers in Bosnia-Herzegovina. Prisoners of conscience are jailed and tortured by government forces in Sudan.

Yet at the same time we all know that violence is only one face and, we believe, not the most important face of religion turned toward the question of human rights. We know that religious traditions have in our time also produced some of the most courageous and persistent pacifists and advocates of human rights: Gandhi, the Dalai Lama, Martin Luther King, Jr., Mother Teresa, among many others. We also know that the teachings of these religions are replete with affirmations of the dignity of human beings and human responsibilities to respect and to preserve human life. But both religious leaders and human rights advocates are often puzzled about just where to find these positive resources and how to make the best use of them in the current struggle to defend human life and dignity against their various assailants.

The purpose of this paper is to provide some guidance to those who wish to engage in a search for such resources. We make no effort here to obscure the lamentable fact that throughout history religions have frequently incited and exacerbated human conflicts; but we also insist that, rightly understood, religious traditions can provide indispensable sources of moral instruction, inspiration, and imagery that can be used to advance inter-group understanding and promote human solidarity. We suggest at the outset that in searching for such resources the inquirer should remember that religious traditions are vast and complex. They resist simplification into slogans. Still, if one goes to the core ideas, central values of human dignity and well-being, basic scriptures, most powerful images, exemplary persons, and key interpreters in these traditions, a wealth of constructive material can be found. We further believe that, given the unfortunate tendency of the mass media to accentuate the negative and to focus on the most divisive features of the world's religions, it is urgent for those of us who are familiar with the other side to make every effort to bring this positive material to light and use it to the best advantage.

Several documents constitute what is now called the International Bill of Human Rights. For the sake of economy, we have chosen only one of them, the Universal Declaration of Human Rights, to illustrate the thesis of this paper.[1] Adopted by the United Nations General Assembly in 1948, the Declaration is the foundation on which all subsequent international human rights agreements are based.

Three theses are possible in relation to the contention that religions provide positive resources for human rights: (1) When religions are used as resources, they can *enlarge* the scope of human rights. For instance, according to Article 3 of the Universal Declaration, "Everyone has the right to life, liberty and security of person." When religions such as Hinduism, Buddhism, and Jainism, as well as indigenous traditions, are used as illustrative resources on this point, the extension of the right to life beyond human life is suggested. Other forms of life, especially animal life, or even the treatment of plants, may be encompassed by this extension.[2] (2) When religions are used as resources, they bring to light the *interrelation* among the various articles of the Declaration. Under the Sharī'a, for instance, compelling need mitigates the punishment for theft.[3] This principle leads to a reading of Article 17, on the right of property ownership, in the light of Article 25, on adequate living standards, rather than a more isolated reading. (3) When religions are used as resources, they can *strengthen* the concept of human rights as it is usually formulated and understood.

---

[1] For the texts of these documents, see *Human Rights: The International Bill of Human Rights* (New York: United Nations, 1993), which includes the Universal Declaration of Human Rights; the International Covenant on Economic, Social and Cultural Rights; and the International Covenant on Civil and Political Rights and Optional Protocols.

[2] See, e.g., M.K. Gankhi, *Hindu Dharma*, Bharatan Kumarappa, ed., (Ahmedabad: Navajivan Press, 1950), pp. 169-71, 188-200; Akira Hirakawa, "Ahimsā" in G. P. Malalasekera, ed., *Encyclopedia of Buddhism* I (Colombo: Government of Ceylon, 1961, p. 288; P. S. Jaini, *The Jaina Path of Purification* (Berkeley: University of California Press, 1979), pp. 167-69, 304-06, 311-15; and *Manusmṛti* VIII: 285-86.

[3] For this point we are indebted to a personal communication from Professor M. Hallaq, Institute of Islamic Studies, McGill University.

This paper is concerned only with the third thesis: that religions can serve as a positive resource for strengthening human rights as we currently understand them. We shall proceed to illustrate this thesis by dealing with the following question: How does one identify positive resources of religions for human rights as presently conceived? The exercise can be reduced to three dimensions: *What* are we looking for? *Where* do we look for it? And *how* do we look for it? What we are looking for is most easily identified. We are looking for correlations between religious traditions and the thirty articles of the Universal Declaration of Human Rights. Inasmuch as human rights are grounded in human dignity, however, we are looking at religions not just for affirmations of human rights that can be documented, but also for positive constructions of human dignity.

WHERE TO LOOK

There are at least three main dimensions of a religious tradition which may be examined for examples of human rights affirmation: the historical, the social, and the scriptural. In other words, the loci of positive resources consist of the historical, social, and scriptural backgrounds and expressions of the various religions.

Historical Dimension

Three levels of this dimension can be identified: the classical formulations of the traditions, modern reformist movements within the traditions, and contemporary developments in the traditions.

Classical Formulations. Even in their classical formulations, anticipations of human rights can be identified within the various traditions. As already noted, in Hinduism, Buddhism, and Jainism, for example, the abjuration of taking life goes far beyond the right to life enshrined in Article 3 of the Universal Declaration. Similarly, freedom of movement and residence realized within traditional Hinduism exceeded the provisions of Article 13 ("Everyone has the right to freedom of movement and residence within the borders of each state"), and Hinduism's preservation of cultural differences exceeded Article 22 ("Everyone, as a member of society, has the right to social security and is entitled to realization...of the economic, social and cultural rights indispensable for his dignity and the free development of his personality"). According to the testimony of a Jesuit traveler to southern India in the early decades of the 19th century:

Although amalgamated in some degree, each of these tribes still preserves to the present day the language and mode of life peculiar to the place from which it originally sprang. The same thing may be remarked throughout the Peninsula but especially in the Tamil country and in Mysore, where many families of Telugus are to be found whose ancestors were obliged for various reasons to quit their native soil and migrate thither. The remembrance of their original birthplace is engraved on the hearts of these Telugus, and they always carefully avoid following the peculiar usages of their adoptive country. Yet they are invariably treated with the perfect tolerance. Indeed, every native of India is quite free to take up his abode wherever it may seem good to him. Nobody will quarrel with him for living his own life, speaking what language he pleases, or following whatever customs he is used to. All that is asked of him is that he should conform generally to the accustomed rules of decorum recognized in the neighbourhood.[1]

Further, traditional Hindu law allows a woman to actively seek a husband on her own if her parents fail her in this respect.[2] The right of Hindu women to own property accords well with Clause 1 of Article 17 ("Everyone has the right to own property alone as well as in association with others"). Contrary to popular belief, the *lex talionis* ("an eye for an eye") does not imply that we can go about gouging each others' eyes, but rather enshrines the principle of compensation in Jewish law. According to this understanding, the *lex talionis* goes even beyond Clause 2 of Article 17 ("No one shall be arbitrarily deprived of his property"), for the Universal Declaration contains no provision for compensation for the violation of this right.[3]

The following Hindu example of freedom of religion, guaranteed under Article 18, *within a family* is also worth remarking:

In some parts a remarkable peculiarity is to be observed in reference to these two sects. Sometimes the husband is a Vishnavite and bears the namam on his forehead, while the wife is a follower of Siva and wears the lingam. The former eats meat, but the latter may not touch it. This divergency of religious opinion, however, in no way destroys the peace of the household. Each observes the practices of his or her own particular creed, and worships his or her god in the way that seems best, without any interference from the other.[4]

---

[1] J.A. Dubois, *Hindu Manners, Customs, and Ceremonies,* H. K. Beauchamp, ed. and trans., (Oxford: Clarendon University Press, 1959), pp. 11-12.

[2] See Huston Smith, *The World's Religions* (San Francisco: Harper & Row, 1933), p. 251, and *Manusmṛti* IX: 93, as well as *Mahābhārata* III: 32-33.

[3] Again, see *Manusmṛti* III: 51. Exodus 21:23-25. It should be noted that the international human rights Covenant on Civil and Political Rights, adopted in 1966, does provide for the "enforceable right to compensation."

[4] Dubois, *Hindu Manners,* p. 119.

Many have attested to the manifest demonstration of human equality during Hajj, the sacred pilgrimage of Islam. Malcolm X, for example, describes its epic egalitarian grandeur in his *Autobiography*:

> There were tens of thousands of pilgrims, from all over the world. They were of all colors, from blue-eyed blondes to black-skinned Africans. But we were all participating in the same ritual, displaying a spirit of unity and brotherhood that my experiences in America had led me to believe never could exist between the white and the non-white.
>
> America needs to understand Islam, because this is the one religion that erases from its society the race problem. Throughout my travels in the Muslim world, I have met, talked to, and even eaten with people who in America would have been considered 'white'—but the 'white' attitude was removed from their minds by the religion of Islam. I have never before seen *sincere* and *true* brotherhood practiced by all colors together, irrespective of their color....
>
> During the past eleven days here in the Muslim world, I have eaten from the same plate, drank from the same glass, and slept in the same bed (or on the same rug)—while praying to the *same* God—with fellow Muslims, whose eyes were the bluest of blue, whose hair was the blondest of blond, and whose skin was the whitest of white. And in the *words* and in the *actions* and in the *deeds* of the 'white' Muslims, I felt the same sincerity that I felt among the black African Muslims of Nigeria, Sudan, and Ghana.
>
> We were truly all the same.[1]

It is clear from the preceding illustrations that various religions can provide positive examples of the affirmation of what we now call human rights and of the concept of human dignity which underlies human rights.

Reform Movements. Reform movements within religions provide even more striking illustrations of this affirmation. The manner in which Reform Judaism has promoted gender equality is well known. In relation to Islam, we may consider the view of the Sudanese Muslim reformer Ustadh Mahmoud Mohamed Taha, who suggested that "the early process of abrogation (*naskh*) should now be reversed in order to implement the verses of the Qur'an which enjoin freedom of religion and equality between all human beings regardless of gender or religious faith."[2] We also need to take into account the fact that Mahatma Gandhi instituted fundamental changes within Hinduism by reordering its axiological priorities, by emphasizing duties common to all (*sādhāraṇa*

---

[1] Malcolm X, *The Autobiography of Malcolm X* (New York: Grove Press, 1965), p. 345.
[2] Abdullahi Ahmed An-Na'im, "Qur'an, Shari'a and Human Rights: Foundations, Deficiencies and Prospects," in Hans Küng and Jurgen Moltmann, eds., *The Ethics of World Religions and Human Rights* (London: SCM Press, 1990), p. 67.

dharmas), such as truthfulness, over duties specific to one's station in society and stage in life (*varnāśramadharmas*). The revolutionary potential of reformist Islam and Hinduism as positive resources for human rights seems undeniable.[1] In fact, it may be misleading to use the word "reform," for what is being attempted is the amplification of the tradition to enlarge its original insights. An illustration from Western culture might help. The Magna Carta received royal assent in 1215. By the 19th century, perhaps through working out the biblical implications of human dignity implicit in its drafting, this document had led to "a doctrine of universal human rights, even if it was not clear in practice whether it applied to *black men as well as white men, and to women as well as men.*"[2] Similarly, today's movements for black civil rights and women's rights are the expanding, even explosive, moral universes released in 1776 by the original "big bang" of the American Declaration of Independence. These movements represent steps toward realization of the full potential of the Declaration.

Gender discrimination in religious roles and functions is invidious from the point of view of human rights. Religious reform movements, by promoting its removal, are generally well placed to give a fillip to the human rights movement because of the high profile religious functionaries enjoy, especially in traditional societies. The Anglican Church's recent ordination of women and the trend in Hinduism for women to assume priestly roles are additional steps toward achieving the goal of equal rights for men and women that is enshrined in the preamble to the Universal Declaration of Human Rights.[3]

The question of the Western origins of the concept of human rights also must be addressed. In this context, it is sometimes suggested that the religions of the Western world tend to speak in terms of "rights," while those of the Eastern world speak in terms of "duties." If this suggestion proves accurate, we must ask whether religions of the East can be a positive resource in the context of human rights.

Contemporary Developments. This question is more easily answered in a contemporary than an historical context. During the age of Western imperialism, masses were mobilized against powerful Western nations, the end of whose political and military domination was not in sight. Emphasis on "duty for duty's sake" made sense in the struggle against this domination, even if peoples were fighting for their political *right* to freedom. Using religion as a positive resource

---

[1] See, e.g., Abdullahi Ahmed An-Na'im, *Toward an Islamic Reformation: Civil Liberties, Human Rights and International Law* (Syracuse: Syracuse University Press, 1990).
[2] J. B. Carman, "Duties and Rights in Hindu Societies" in L. S. Rounder, ed., *Human Rights and the World's Religions* (Notre Dame: University of Notre Dame Press, 1988), pp. 113-28; quotation from p. 117 (emphasis added).
[3] See, e.g., "Mistress of Ceremonies" in *India Today*, March 31, 1994, p. 13.

by aligning with its emphasis on "duty" also made sense in this struggle. But now that most of the erstwhile colonies are independent nations, "rights" which independence struggles were carried out to secure no longer can be ignored. Even if religious traditions emphasize duties over rights, emphasis *can* be shifted. Hinduism, for example, has shifted its emphasis within the last two centuries from an other-worldly to a this-worldly asceticism.

Moreover, suitable analogues to rights may exist in other traditions. As John Carman points out,

> It is worth noting that our Western notion of rights goes back much further than the affirmation of *equal rights*. What is one's right is what is one's due, whether it is because of who one is by birth or because of what one had accomplished. It is one's fair share even if it is not an equal share. That notion of right is deeply embedded in the Hindu social system [in which the concept of *ṛta* or what is due to the gods, sages, and ancestors from one can be easily transformed into what is due *to* one].[1]

The common word for God in Hinduism, *Bhagavān*, may plausibly mean one to whom something is due. The word for "religion" in Arabic, *al-dīn*," is said by some grammarians of Arabic and by some Qur'anic commentators to derive from *al-dayn*, which means debt. *Al-dīn*, therefore, is the repaying of one's debt to God."[2] Apart from providing a prospective point of intersection between Hinduism and Islam, the idea of "debt to God" has only to be reversed in moving from God to the state to yield the concept of what is due to someone (as opposed to due from him or her) to become symmetrical with the modern concept of rights.[3] Religion, then, is genuinely an element in the formation of political groupings' identities.

Religion also can be cynically manipulated to reinforce and even to generate conflict. These facts immensely complicate the relationship between religion and human rights in modern times. However, most religious traditions contain both a

---

[1] Carman, "Duties and Rights," p. 121. Bracketed text is our own interpolation.

[2] S. H. Nasr, "Islam" in Arvind Sharma, ed., *Our Religions* (San Francisco: Harper & Row, 1993), quotation from p. 439.

[3] This issue may, however, call for exploration in greater depth. Many post-colonial countries are not yet nation-states as such, but they are in the process of emerging as nation-states with strong, well-defined governments. Inasmuch as human rights are asserted against the "powers of the state," the issue becomes especially problematic. The severe punishment for apostasy in Islam may be related to a similar predicament. On the general point, see John Mohawk, "The Pre-existence of Human Rights: Its Subversion by the Western State," *Interculture* 83 (April-June 1984): 74-77; on the Islamic context, see, e.g., Riffat Hassan, "On Human Rights and the Qur'anic Perspective" in Arlene Swidler, ed., *Human Rights in Religious Traditions* (New York: Pilgrim Press, 1982), especially p. 61.

particularist and a universalist dimension. The role of a religion in the context of human rights will depend to a large extent on which dimension prevails. In fact, juxtaposing human rights and a particular religious tradition may help a faith community to focus more on the universalist dimension.

Social Dimension

Of all dimensions of a religion, its social dimension is usually regarded as most problematic in relation to human rights. Yet one must avoid premature pessimism in the area of reconciliation. In order to justify cautious optimism, we will provide concrete instances of how socio-legal structures associated with certain religious traditions can undergo revision to become more supportive of human rights. The developments which led to such a creative revisioning within Christianity have been extensively documented. Less well known is the suggestion of the famous Indian Muslim thinker Muhammad Iqbal that the end of verbal prophecy in Islam implies that human beings are to take charge of their own destiny. This claim is of a piece with the claim to the right of *Ijtihād* or fresh interpretation of revelation in a modern context as a source of Islamic law.[1] More concretely, we will try to demonstrate that even the Hindu caste system can be reconciled with or made "user-friendly" in terms of human rights principles.

Popular impressions suggest that nothing could be more antithetical to human rights than caste. Yet the Indian Constitution and the Indian political system made strange bedfellows of the two. Let us not pronounce them divorced even before their marriage, notwithstanding the obstacles to consummation.

Our first task is to make the caste system intelligible—neither acceptable nor damnable, but simply intelligible—to Western and Westernized Indian readers. As the raison d'etre of caste is birth-ascription, we ask the reader the following question: Which cultural (as distinguished from natural) dimension of human existence in the West is defined by birth?

The answer is evident: nationality. In the West one's national citizenship is just as firmly based on birth as caste is. This concept is almost religiously binding. Couples from Hong Kong have been known to travel to Canada, with the wife in advanced pregnancy, so that their child could be born in Canada. The child is then a natural citizen who can, upon reaching the designated age, sponsor his or her parents as immigrants! Birth-ascribed nationality can make a child "the father of the man" in a way Wordsworth did not imagine. It is worth noting that a child born to U.S. citizens in the United Kingdom is automatically a

---

[1] Allama Muhammad Iqbal, *The Reconstruction of Religious Thought in Islam* (Lahore: Iqbal Academy Pakistan and Institute of Islamic Culture, 1989), pp. 100-01.

British citizen, even if the parents are not entitled to hold British passports. Such is the miracle of birth in modern polity. Although citizenship can be acquired, birth still has priority, as shown in eligibility requirements for the U.S. presidency. Note that the place of birth, then, constitutes a *political* space.

A citizen of a country is likely to marry a citizen of the same country and is likely to mix primarily, although not exclusively, with fellow-citizens of that country when overseas. In other words, the circle of connubium and commensality tends to be constituted by one's nationality, just as in the case of caste. To a lesser extent, one's predilection toward a certain career-orientation is often associated with nationality, as revealed by expressions such as Yankee ingenuity, German technology, British diplomacy, etc. Nationality thus provides the proper analogue for caste with this important difference: the place of birth, in terms of caste, constitutes a *social* space.

We shall return to this important distinction between political and social space, but first let us consider some similarities. Notwithstanding the hierarchy *among* castes, all are born equal *within* a caste. There is perfect democracy, and one is even judged by one's peers. Caste constitutes one's social security net, just as the nation, with its social services, constitutes a citizen's safety net. Indians have no social security number; they have their caste.

The popular imagination, especially in the West, overwhelmingly connects caste and hierarchy within a society. The case of nations is similar, however, yet outside each nation. Nations rise to and fall from power. Political pundits who speak of a Third and Fourth World are merely replicating the fourfold *varna* or class order of Hinduism, which subsumes all castes, just as the four "worlds" subsume all the countries of the world. Consider that India perceived itself as the world to such an extent that no classical Hindu "universal" monarch stepped outside India, prevented from doing so, we are assured by the Greeks, "out of a sense of justice." The *varna* system, said to be characteristic of such an India, was equated with the world.

A conclusion emerges in that both citizenship and caste membership are determined by birth, although differences develop when this shared starting point is applied in terms of *society* or in terms of *polity*. When applied societally, the birth determinant gives rise to the caste system. When applied politically, it gives rise to the nation-state. In both Indian and Western societies, the principle of birth determination was applied at a particular point in time. This point is unknown in the case of India. In the West it followed the Reformation. Application of the principle produced comparable results, in keeping with its respective social and political idiom. Being stateless and being casteless are comparable misfortunes.

The emergence of India as a nation provides an important illustration. To begin with, the weakness of the Indian concept of nation-state has often been remarked. However, when large numbers of people are organized as a society in terms of caste, many of the functions of a state come to be handled socially. Such functions include, to some extent, aspects of the administration of justice. Empires rise and fall; society continues, as it has in India. Whence follows the inadequate politicization of a people, from a modern point of view, and the weakness of national feeling. Second, while politically organized groups are involved in an *external* hierarchy of nations, socially organized groups based on caste are involved in an *internal* hierarchy. The former is fluid, and the latter is more or less fixed, at least in broad terms and for longer periods than the political eras of nations. Third, the direct relationship between the citizen and the state is mediated by a caste in societies organized by caste. In India today the competing ideal of a nation has been placed alongside caste, although both are based on birth. The government is attempting to convert all Indians into one caste: the Indian caste, as it were.

India is caught, then, in the shift from "society" to "polity." Inasmuch as the latter form of organization is very different from the former, India seems adrift. However, inasmuch as both are based on birth, India possesses a "home ground" advantage. In cases of both caste system and nation-state, the scale has created the phenomenon, and the basis of the phenomenon in both cases is birth ascription. This example, we hope, illustrates that when the principles of otherwise apparently antithetical systems are uncovered, radical revision may be possible. A scalar shift in the operational locus of the basic premise of the caste system renders it "rights-friendly." Do I not destroy my enemy, Abraham Lincoln is believed to have asked, if I make him [or her] a friend?

Scriptural Dimension

The following are some of the passages invoked from various traditions in discussions of human rights:

Judaism:
> For in the image of God was man created. *Genesis 1:27*

Judaism and Christianity:
> Thou shalt love thy neighbor as thyself. *Leviticus 19:18, Matthew 22:39*

Islam:
> Let there be no compulsion in religion. *Sura 2:256*

Hinduism:
> The truth is one, and sages call it by various names. *Ṛg Veda I.164.46*

Buddhism:
> For hatred does not cease by hatred at any time:
> hatred ceases by love, this is an old rule.   *Dhammapada 1.5*

Confucianism:
> Then all within the four seas will be his brothers.   *Analects 12.5*

Taoism:
> Peace is the highest value.   *Tao Te Ching, Chap. 31*

Iroquois:
> All peoples shall love one another and live together in peace.   *Book of Life*

Maori:
> Who will care and caress this land, this earth?...
> It is truth, justice, and compassion.   *Traditional Maori song*

These passages may seem to be in the nature of ideal affirmations of human dignity and of the aspirations underlying the Universal Declaration of Human Rights. This observation, however, does not diminish their importance for the distinctive contribution of religion to the cause of human rights. Many scholars have demonstrated how each tradition could utilize its scriptural resources to further the cause of human rights.[1] We suggest that virtually every religious tradition articulates in one way or another a basic conviction about the unity of the human family. The theistic traditions symbolize this unity in terms of a single Creator. Other traditions make the same point in other ways. But however articulated, this conviction remains one of the principal bulwarks in religious traditions against inter-group fratricide. These same traditions, again in their own various ways, emphasize the unique value of each person. The fact that human life is seen within the larger context of a divine or cosmic order is a reminder of this conviction. Many more examples of scriptural contributions to human rights could be added.

HOW TO LOOK

As will be obvious from the preceding discussion, identification within religions of positive resources for human rights is not enough. Subsequent to locating positive resources, issues must be raised and distinctions drawn related to the question of how to look at religions as positive resources.

---

[1] See, e.g., Swidler, *Human Rights*; Rouner, *Human Rights*; Küng and Moltmann, *Ethics of World Religions*; and Robert Traer, *Faith in Human Rights: Support in Religious Traditions for a Global Struggle* (Washington, D.C.: Georgetown University Press, 1991).

We believe it is critical, in searching the various expressions of these traditions, to distinguish between the major thrust of a tradition and its minor or transient expressions. It is essential to call upon the best informed scholarly work available and not to rely on shallow media reports. Students of the Qur'an or of the Hindu tradition would immediately insist, for example, that those who call for the death of a writer or the destruction of a mosque, allegedly in the name of their tradition, cannot substantiate their demands from the main thrust of the tradition. Christians have to ask whether Innocent III, who preached the crusades, or St. Francis, who tried to stop them, was closer to the core of the Christian message.

We also believe it is essential to make a clear distinction between, on the one hand, human conflicts caused principally by religiously based hostilities and, on the other, human conflicts springing from other sources of tension (e.g., economic class or national identity) but exacerbated rather than mitigated by religious loyalties. It is particularly important in assessing religious resources for overcoming human rights violations to scrutinize certain main threads in a tradition. Such threads include teachings about the position of women; the care of children; and responsibilities to the poor, the outsider, the sick, the stranger, and the prisoner. These are people who often lack power in society and who often have been special subjects of religiously based ethical concern. Too often, however, secondary customs and derivative practices which have not been drawn from the heart of the tradition are misused against the less powerful. In our time it is especially important, we believe, to separate the core teachings of religions from secondary additions referring to the status of women, as, for example, Muslim and Christian women are now doing. We also believe that the compassion religious traditions frequently commend for homeless people and for refugees are especially critical in this moment of history.

IMPORTANT DISTINCTIONS

The following distinctions must be borne in mind in assessing the role of religions in the context of human rights: (i) between appearance and reality, (ii) between duties and rights, (iii) between theory and practice, (iv) between legality and morality, and (v) between the whole and parts—that is, between religions serving as resources for human rights in terms of individual aspects of the religion, in terms of a moral system in which the individual aspect is embedded, and in terms of the religious traditions of the world treated collectively rather than individually.

Appearance vs. Reality

An apparently positive example of the convergence of religion and human rights may not, in fact, bear scrutiny. The fact that under Hindu law even a woman charged with adultery may not be denied financial support has a positive ring to it, but the provision is based on a negative assessment of her character.[1] Similarly, the declaration that "all people are created equal" might do well as a *deistic* statement, but it is not so unclouded as a *theistic* statement. In some post-lapsarian Christian theological contexts, all people may not be redeemed equally.

Duties vs. Rights

The need for thoughtful subtlety may extend further. Sometimes religions glory in their loftiness. For example, Hinduism's ideal of selfless action has been hailed as an ideal not only for India, but also for the world. Louis Renou writes:

> Ambivalence is characteristic of India: for her, what is the good of killing her cows if she has to lose her soul? A factor in social and psychical equilibrium is found in the notion of *dharma* with its rigorous justice and the 'truth' which it implies (the Indians insist on the attitude of truthfulness as others insist on an 'attitude of consciousness'). An important consequence of this is tolerance, nonviolence considered an active virtue; this is a manner of acting which must be respected—even in the political sphere—*regardless of the attitude of others*. In this perhaps is to be found the most spectacular contribution which India has made to the modern world and the most worthy reply to Marxism and its materialism.[2]

This passage would incline one to favor duties over rights in a Hindu context. Some moralists also argue that the idioms of rights and duties are interchangeable, since someone's right is also someone's duty, and vice versa. Therefore, one could continue to favor the idiom of duties over the idiom of rights. However, the rights idiom may still possess an advantage from the perspective of human rights protection. For instance, the gospel of selfless action in Hinduism, which emphasizes duty for duty's sake (as in the *Bhagavadgītā*), is vulnerable to cynical exploitation through rejection of any claim to rights by people who are exploited. The exploiters direct the discourse back to duties! Emphasis on rights may provide a bulwark against such deontological exploitation, especially at a time when the tradition's religious vogue has

---

[1] P.V. Kane, *History of Dharmaśāstra* II (Poona: Bhandarkar Oriental Research Institute, 1974), Part I, pp. 572-73.

[2] Louis Renou, *Hinduism* (New York: George Braziller, 1962), pp. 55-56.

become *karmayoga*—that is, the doctrine that one should perform one's duty regardless of fruits that accrue from its performance.

Exponents of some religious traditions have argued that "rights follow from duties discharged." One can identify at least three valid points implicit in this statement: (i) that reckless insistence on rights is thereby checked; (ii) that duties have a logical priority over rights, in the sense that unless fulfilling a right is someone's duty, that right leads a vaporous existence; and (iii) that rights and duties go together, and one does not exclude consideration of the other. However, the implications of the statement can be properly operational only in a situation where rights have already been secured. Inasmuch as current human rights struggles are directed toward securing these rights, emphasis on the inalienable character of the rights seems more desirable. In the various religious traditions this inalienable character is affirmed in terms of human dignity and worth.

Theory vs. Practice

The distinction between theory and practice also must be constantly kept in mind. For instance, some scholars have argued not only that the generous spirit of the Qur'an is inconsistent with slavery, but also that slavery was meant to be prohibited by the Qur'an.[1] The majority view differs, and slavery persisted for centuries in Islam, as in Christianity despite the injunction to "love the neighbor as thyself." Hindu texts vigorously condemn the sale of a daughter, yet a dowry system emerged in India.[2] Even if an ideal is only honored when it is breached, its very presence as an ideal provides a potentially important resource within a tradition that should not be disregarded.

Law vs. Morality

Not merely the idealism, but also the moral ideas addressed by religion are important. These ideas can constitute a double-edged sword in a human rights context, however, and the line drawn by a tradition between law and morality represents one such case. At one extreme, all law may be considered divine law, thereby virtually collapsing the distinction between legality and morality. At the other pole, the two may be quite separable, as in a secular Christian society. In between these extremes fall concepts of "natural law," law of karma, etc. A positive resource for human rights in religion might be a concept of natural law, provided such a concept could be identified in all religions.

---

[1] *Sura* 24:33; 4:92; 5:89; 9:60; 58:3; 2:177; see also Hassan, "On Human Rights," p. 59.
[2] *Manusmṛti* III: 51-54; IX:98-100.

The entry on "natural law" in the *Encyclopedia of Religion* upholds, on the one hand, the link between the doctrine of natural law and human rights but fails to provide references, on the other, for natural law or its analogues in any non-Western religious tradition, including Confucianism.[1] The following issues, therefore, must be addressed: (1) Can a concept of natural law be identified in all religions (even after being "problematized" in terms of the difficulty of discerning what the concept is and who should define it)? and (2) Should natural law be used as a positive resource for human rights in either a limited or general way? The point is that if human rights represent a code of conduct appropriate to a disclosure of natural law interpreted as human nature, then are religious resources relevant? These resources may still be relevant in undergirding humanism, but one must bear in mind the fact that secular humanism could achieve the same results that religious humanism could.

However, there is nothing to prevent these two forms of humanism—secular and religious—from converging. It is, in fact, possible to view human rights as the finest moral expression of modern secularism *and* as analogous to, say, the Ten Commandments. The relationship between law and morals within a religion may serve as a positive intellectual resource for addressing human rights; the concept of human rights itself can and has been related to both law and morals; and human rights share the creative ambiguities which characterize the relationship between the two.

Whole vs. Parts

Any measure taken in relation to a moral system may be judged in the light of whether it makes the moral system (a) possible, (b) credible, or (c) estimable.[2] Moral systems are made *possible* when, for example, individuals keep their promises, honor reciprocal obligations (of which the former point is only one example), and respect the authority of moral standards (of which the previous point is an example). Similarly, moral systems are made *credible* by regulating family patterns (e.g., through incest taboos and care of children), identifying responsibilities of adult members, establishing normative control over the exercise of violence, and establishing normative standards for the exchange of

---

[1] Douglas Sturm, "Natural Law" in Eliade, *Encyclopedia of Religion*, vol. 10, pp. 318-24; also see Surabhji Sheth, "Equality and Inequality in Hindu Scriptures" in R. Siriwardena, ed., *Equality and the Religious Traditions of Asia* (London: Frances Printer, 1987), pp. 21-50 (especially p. 26); and Karen Turner, "War, Punishment, and the Law of Nature in Early Chinese Concepts of the State," *Harvard Journal of Asiatic Studies* 52/2 (December 1993): pp. 285-324.

[2] Frederick Bird, "Moral Universals," *Journal of Religious Pluralism* 3 (1993):29-82, especially pp. 48-77.

valued goods. Finally, moral systems are made *estimable* by justifying or defending the system rationally, aiming at the common good, promoting acceptance of individual moral responsibility, and articulating concepts of inalienable human rights.

This analysis provides a heuristic for identifying the loci which will enable a religion to function as a positive resource for human rights when the latter are not merely treated as a legal entity, but are also perceived as grounded in human dignity and as promoting justice.[1] Any doctrine or practice found in, or emanating from, any religion could be assessed in terms of whether it renders human rights possible, credible, or estimable. This heuristic can be applied at three levels: to particular items within a tradition, to the entire moral or legal systems of the tradition, and to any universal ethic that could be derived from all religions of the world.

A GLOBAL APPROACH

The recent attempt to frame a global ethic may be seen as an effort to identify a universal moral system from the religious perspective. If this ethic is perceived as a foil to the Universal Declaration of Human Rights, a similar moral system from the secular side, the question arises: Do human rights need to be grounded in anything outside of a secular moral system? If our answer to this question is in the affirmative, then the initial declaration of a "Global Ethic" at the 1993 Parliament of the World's Religions is a step in the right direction.[2]

This exploration should be continued. The reasons for excluding "God" from the declaration go beyond Buddhist objections and points to a prouder and profounder truth about human nature: moral consciousness is more universal than theistic consciousness. Moreover, Confucians would point out that the emergence of law itself signifies the failure of morality, although law seeks its roots in morality, and that moral consciousness is more pervasive than legal consciousness. Indigenous peoples too speak of an expansive moral consciousness that includes not only human well-being, but also the flourishing of all living beings within an interdependent environment.

The need to maintain a global perspective in the context of human rights is necessary not only because human beings are found around the globe and everyone should be represented in human rights discussions, but also because certain

---

[1] See, e.g., Traer, *Faith in Human Rights*, p. 2.
[2] See, e.g., Traer, *Faith in Human Rights*, p. 52; Hans Küng and Karl-Josef Kuschel, eds., *A Global Ethic: The Declaration of the Parliament of the World's Religions* (New York: Continuum, 1993). The latter contains the text of the parliamentary declaration.

phenomena can be fully comprehended only on a global scale, e.g., the environmental crisis. Religious perspectives enable us to see human beings within a more inclusive vision of life.[1] A global approach may also help to identify religions collectively as positive resources for human rights. Such a collective resource may be qualitatively different from the resources provided by religions individually. For instance, the intriguing possibility arises that "differing cultures can arrive at a similar conclusion about rights by rather different routes—some via explicit philosophizing, as with Locke, Kant and others in the West; others by contemplating religious texts and duties (the Mīmāṁsā and the *Gītā*); others again by exploiting ideas of ritual and performative behavior toward others (e.g., *li* in China as a source of rights)."[2] As one assesses and compares religious traditions, it sometimes becomes clear that there are genuine and not simply spurious or derivative elements of difference among them. It is important to ask some key questions: First, how much is this difference actually emphasized, by whom, and under what circumstances? Secondly, are there indications that sources of disagreement can be discussed and possibly even modified? If such modification seems unlikely, is there any reason why disagreement in one area must prevent cooperation in another? Religious traditions exist within history. They are not eternally closed; they change, often in response to each other. Differences, therefore, should be neither glossed over nor elevated into significance they do not merit. What we are looking for, after all, are the many, many areas in which we can find some agreement, and in which our united voices will do far more than our individual voices to buttress human rights and human dignity.

CONCLUSION

Each religion can claim to have made, or to be making, a special contribution as a positive resource for some dimension of human rights. This claim does not deny the possibility that a religion may contribute generally to all dimensions. Hinduism stakes a claim in relation to freedom of thought, conscience, and religion (see Article 18 of the Universal Declaration); Buddhism stakes a claim by providing the earliest example of institutionalized democratic procedures within the *saṅgha* (see Article 2); Confucianism, with its commitment to education implied in the very term *Ju-chia*, in relation to the right to education (see Article 26); Taoism in relation to recognizing the role of the community (see Article

---

[1] On this point, see, e.g., Küng and Moltmann, *Ethics of World Religions,* pp. 128-33.
[2] Ninian Smart and Shivesh Thakur, eds., *Ethical and Political Dilemmas of Modern India* (New York: St. Martin's Press, 1993), p. xi.

29); Judaism, through its emphasis on the sabbath, promoting the right to rest (see Article 24), and, by its very existence, promoting minority rights (see Article 22); Christianity in relation to the right of association through its concept of ecclesia (see Article 20); Islam in relation to human equality (see Articles 1 and 2); and indigenous traditions in relation to the social and cultural rights indispensable for human dignity (see Article 22).[1]

Religions can continue to contribute positively to human rights. Given the role of religion in conflicts around the world, resolutions should continue to be sought through organizations such as the World Council of Churches, World Conference on Religion and Peace, Fellowship of Reconciliation, Vatican Commission on Justice and Peace, International Association for Religious Freedom, etc. These organizations mobilize religious leaders, groups, and followers of various religions in advocating peaceful methods of conflict resolution. More specifically, in relation to human rights, each religion could be used as a unit for monitoring human rights, much as regions are now the units used by, for example, Human Rights Watch/Africa and Human Rights Watch/Asia. Such a designation could do much to convince the members of a religious tradition that the human rights movement intends to work with them, not against them. A Hindu or Buddhist or Muslim or Sikh human rights monitoring unit might possess three dimensions: (1) a focus on cases where members of a tradition have been denied human rights by governments or quasi-governmental authorities, (2) a focus on cases where members of a tradition have been deprived of basic rights by their own co-religionists; and (3) a focus on cases in which religious leaders have deprived others of basic rights. In addition, religious bodies could serve as nongovernmental organizations through which human rights grievances could be vented and brought to the attention of appropriate agencies.

---

[1] In addition to the articles of the Universal Declaration, see also: Bithika Mukherji, "The Foundations of Unity and Equality: A Hindu Understanding of Human Rights" in Küng and Moltmann, eds., *Ethics of World Religions*, especially p. 70; Robert A. Thurman, "Social and Cultural Rights in Buddhism" in Rouner, *Human Rights*, especially p. 149; Tu Wei-ming, "Confucianism" in Sharma, *Our Religions*, especially p. 147; Smith, *World's Religions*, especially p. 155; Xiaogan Liu, "Taoism" in Sharma, *Our Religions*, especially p.144; Daniel F. Polish, "Judaism and Human Rights" in Swidler, *Human Rights*, especially p. 47, and *passim*; Max L. Stackhouse, *Creeds, Society and Human Rights* (Grand Rapids: William B. Eerdmans, 1984), especially p. 20; Roger Garaudy, "Human Rights and Islam: Foundation, Tradition, Violation," in Küng and Moltmann, eds., *Ethics of World Religions*, especially pp. 47-48; and the United Nations Draft Declaration on the Rights of Indigenous Peoples, as Agreed Upon by the Members of the Working Group (text of this Draft Declaration is reprinted as Appendix B in Alexander Ewen, ed., *Voice of Indigenous Peoples: Native People Address the United Nations* [Santa Fe: Clear Light Publishers, 1994]).

This practical recommendation may be coupled with a suggestion for a more scholarly and educational effort: preparation of a document that identifies and contextualizes from all religions both texts and received traditions which resonate positively with the promotion of human rights and human dignity.

This section was edited by Kusumita P. Pedersen, Executive Director of the Project on Religion and Human Rights. We have been able to include only short excerpts but have made every effort to represent accurately the central concerns of each presenter. Since one of the chief purposes of the meeting was to ask participants to speak from their own experience, we have emphasized this aspect of the discussion when compelled to choose between historical analysis and personal narrative. In this way we have also tried to provide a complement to the preceding papers. We deeply regret that because of an equipment malfunction, the challenging and perceptive presentation of Susannah Heschel in the Interfaith Panel was not recorded and could not be included here.

The symbol §§§ indicates a break in the original transcript.

5

The Dialogue on Religion and Human Rights

On May 22-24, 1994, the Project on Religion and Human Rights convened
the Meeting for Briefing and Evaluation in New York City. One hundred and
thirty people from twenty countries, in addition to the United States, took part.
They included professionals from human rights organizations, religious leaders
of several traditions, public policy experts, writers, scholars and educators, interfaith officers, indigenous leaders, members of nongovernmental organizations, and United Nations staff. The conference had several specific aims: to test
the content of the four preceding studies against the expertise and practical experience of the participants, to gather recommendations for the future work of
the Project, and to explore the differences and commonalities of views about
human rights. The Project's goal was to create effective collaboration and
dialogue.

The meeting heard formal addresses in the opening session, followed by pan-
els of "witnesses" directly involved in current issues confronting four regions:
former Yugoslavia, the Middle East, South Asia, and the United States. All conference participants worked together in small groups before reconvening for
open discussion at the final plenary. Following are highlights of the formal presentations made in the conference. The meeting was memorable for its intensity
of debate, its passion for the issues shared by those present, and an atmosphere
of constructive dialogue combining blunt disagreement and good will.

KEYNOTE ADDRESS: JOHN SHATTUCK
Assistant Secretary of State for Human Rights
and Humanitarian Affairs, U.S.A.

§§§ The emergence of NGOs around the world is one of the most arresting and exciting developments of the post-Cold War era. The human rights and democracy movements that have arisen throughout the world, through the brave and tireless work of extraordinary and heroic people, have become a force to be reckoned with precisely because the power derives *from* the people. Not only can these movements spotlight abuses, they can do things that no government can do—such as building the institutions of civil society and forging consensus for democracy and human rights within countries that have never had them before.

By far the single most rewarding aspect of my own work as Assistant Secretary of State for Human Rights is the obligation and the opportunity I have had to meet with human rights activists wherever I go. I've met with Mansur Kikhia in Egypt, the extraordinary co-founder of the Arab Organization for Human Rights and who two months ago "disappeared" from Cairo and has not been heard from since. I've met with Haiti's Association de Juristes, an extraordinary group of lawyers who are struggling against enormous odds to monitor human rights abuses in their country and to support those who are trying to escape. I've met with Wei Jingsheng in China, who to some symbolizes the Chinese movement for democracy and human rights in China. I've met with the mothers of Vukovar in Croatia, who weep over the mass grave of their sons, killed in the middle of the night after being told they were being taken to refugee camps. I've met with Monique Mujawamariya of Rwanda, an extraordinary woman who managed to escape from violence through great personal courage and is now leading the effort to try to mobilize international support for work to end the devastation which is going on in her country.

Let me speak for a few moments about Rwanda, because we sit here as a human tragedy in massive proportions is unfolding there. Ten days ago I traveled to that region, and I want to bear witness now to what I saw, because I believe that how we respond to the carnage in Rwanda will have repercussions for the moral and legal fabric of the entire international community. The systematic slaughter of human life in Rwanda taxes the limits of the imagination. Literally hundreds of thousands of innocent men, women, and children have been hunted down and killed in a frenzy of ethnic and political violence instigated by extremists. There are more than a quarter of a million Rwandan refugees in Tanzania alone, and I saw with my own eyes thousands of corpses floating down the rivers on the borders of Rwanda.

The mass murder of civilians did not happen spontaneously. It was fomented by individuals who sought to gain political ends through these hideous means. In Rwanda, and not only there but also in Bosnia, in Haiti, and everywhere that we see mass human rights violations, the international community must investigate and assign responsibility. There are three basic reasons why, and I think they are at the heart of the subject that you will be considering at this conference.

First, unless the leaders of violence are made responsible for their acts, the cycle of retribution will continue and claim more lives. Fixing responsibility on those who have directed acts of mass violence can transform revenge into justice, affirm the rule of law, and mercifully break the cycle of retribution.

Second, an investigation is essential to lift the terrible burden of collective guilt that settles quickly on a society when leaders have directed such terrible violence. If countries are to rebuild themselves, that burden must be lifted, and it can only be lifted through basic justice. Moreover, assigning responsibility enables the international community to differentiate between victims and aggressors, and it helps expunge the cynical illusion that conflicts with an ethnic dimension are hopelessly complex and therefore insoluble.

Finally, an investigation is essential if future crimes are to be deterred. If basic human rights can be massively violated anywhere, especially in a remote and unfamiliar place, every part of the world is fair game for every conceivable form of terror. The bloodshed in Rwanda is a direct challenge to the world's commitment to universal human rights and to the rules that hold ethnically diverse nations together.

The experience of Rwanda demonstrates further what we already know: the long-term prospects for democracy and human rights can be threatened by deeply rooted ethnic, racial, and religious conflict. Indeed, the greatest single challenge to human rights in the world today may be the eruption of such conflict, which ironically has arisen in the immediate wake of the Cold War. For this reason, we believe that any strategy to promote democracy and human rights must contain programs to strengthen conflict resolution, for although democracy ultimately may be the best system for multi-ethnic states and societies, we must address ethnic tensions and their violent aggressions in order for democracy to have a chance to take root. We do not accept the journalistic cliché that religious and ethnic conflicts somehow reflect ancient struggles so deeply rooted in history that they lie beyond the reach of politics and diplomacy. To be sure, religious and ethnic differences have histories, and those histories must be understood if the conflicts are to be addressed. Yet, in the final analysis, these conflicts are often, and perhaps always, political and not only ethnic or religious in nature.

It should be remembered that the individual human being is always the focus, the bearer, of universal human rights. If the rights of the individual are protected, it follows that men and women identified as members of a religious or ethnic group have rights that cannot be abridged simply because they are part of a minority. Democracy must safeguard the rights of minorities precisely because in a democracy, all must be treated equally as individuals before the law, irrespective of their group affiliation or identity.

Religion is never in and of itself the problem. To the contrary, religious traditions have a great role to play in promoting universal values of justice and respect for human dignity in a multitude of forms, languages, and ideas. It is fair to say that the rich dimensions of transcendence, spirituality, and moral critique that religions bring to civil society can be immensely enriching to democratic culture and to the protection of human rights.

Those of us who are active in the human rights movement cannot but revere the moral witness to human rights that has been provided by remarkable religious leaders and followers of many faiths.

In this world of the dawning of the 21st century, we face enormous challenges and great opportunities. We are on the threshold of a new world, but we do not yet know what it will look like. Will it be defined by the great worldwide grassroots movement for democracy and human rights that has made such an enormous impact in so many parts of the globe in such a short time during recent years? Or will it be marked by a long slide into the chaos and conflict, human rights abuses, and repression that we are also witnessing with numbing frequency today? History tells us that things could truly go either way.

But we can make a difference. I believe we have it in our power to make freedom and human rights prevail over slavery and suffering. I will close with the words of Vaclav Havel on this subject : "I am not quite the optimist, because I am not sure that everything ends well. Nor am I a pessimist, because I am not sure that everything ends badly. But I carry hope, and the hope is the belief that freedom has meaning—and that liberty is always worth the struggle."   §§§

READING BY TALAT HALMAN
Former Minister of Culture of Turkey

For those who truly love God and His ways,
all the peoples of the world are brothers and sisters.

I'm not here on earth for strife.
Love is the mission of my life.

We regard no one's religion as contrary to ours.
True love is born when all faiths are united.

These are random couplets from the humanistic poetry of the 13th-century Turkish folk poet, Yunus Emre, who celebrated the supremacy of love, the purity of the mystic spirit, and justice, harmony, and equality among all human beings, peace in the heart, and peace in the world. His passionate plea was for the acumen of ecumenism. His dream world embraced pantheism and the unity of all faiths.

From the mountains and rocks,
I call you out, my God,
With the birds as day breaks,
I call you out, my God.

With Jesus in the sky,
Moses on Mt. Sinai,
Raising my scepter high,
I call you out, my God.

Yunus Emre and other Muslim mystics stressed and gave voice to the liberal spirit of Islam, taking cues from the holy Qur'an's affirmative teachings, from its aspirations of peace and understanding, and also from the Prophet Muhammad's statements. The Prophet Muhammad once said, *"All people are equal, as equal as the teeth of a comb. An Arab is no better than a non-Arab, nor is a white person over a black person, nor is the male superior to the female."*

In the 13th century the eminent Universalist philosopher poet of Islamic mysticism, Mevlana Jallaludin Rumi, issued his eloquent pleas:

Whatever you think of war
I'm far, far from it.
Whatever you think of love,
I'm that, only that, all that.

In all mosques, churches, temples, I find one shrine alone.

Like a compass I stand firm with one leg on my faith,
And roam with the other leg all over the seventy-two nations. §§§

It is for the children of the world that we must keep our dreams alive. The 20th-century Turkish poet, Nazim Hikmet, articulated this vision:

Let's give the world to the children, at least for one day.
Let them play with it as if it's a spangled balloon,
Let them sing and dance among the stars.
Let's give the world to the children like a huge apple,
  or a warm loaf of bread,
  at least for one day, so that they'll have enough to eat.
Let's give the world to the children
  so that even if it's just for one day,
  the world will learn what friendship is.
The children will take the world out of our hands,
  and they will plant immortal trees.

And in the spirit of that poem, I believe in the compelling power of love to give happiness and nobility to our future. I rhapsodize in a poem of my own, entitled "Love Tomorrow":

We shall love tomorrow,
  Red poppies will burst open in a mirage
  Ending the pigeon's night solitude.
Tomorrow we shall laugh,
  Heaven's light will envy our moonbeams,
  Rain will pour up to the sun.

We shall love tomorrow.

Hydrangeas will no longer suffer thirst,
As galleons soar to God with wind and sea.

We shall love tomorrow.

I have faith in the marvels of love; I have faith in faith itself. As I expressed in one of my short poems:

The buried bird, if it has faith,
Takes wing in the ground. §§§

INTERFAITH PANEL
Moderated by Rabbi J. Rolando Matalon
Congregation B'nai Jeshurun

Oren R. Lyons, Chief, Faithkeeper, Onondaga Nation

I am a Faithkeeper of the Turtle Clan of the Onondaga Nation, Firekeepers of the Haudenosaunee, the Iroquois Confederacy. I speak as a representative of one of the many indigenous nations of North America.

I wish to tell you that prior to the landfall of Christopher Columbus and subsequent invasions of our lands by Christians from Europe, we had a well-established understanding of spirit and nature. We understood that life was free and that we had rights as human beings. We also had responsibilities to see that these freedoms were protected. We were instructed that all life is equal, that we must work together and respect this life, that we must be in harmony with all living beings, and that rights are extended to them as well. We call the Earth our Mother because all life comes from her. We believe in the creation of the world by an all-powerful spiritual force that guides the universe. We understand that universal law controls life as we know it and that we, the human beings, are related and intertwined with all life that surrounds us. Hence the Lakotas close all of their prayers with the phrase "All my relations," meaning *all* life.

We were instructed to give thanks for all life forces. To do this we developed ceremonies that are now ancient. We were instructed that when human beings ceased ceremonies of thanksgiving and acknowledgment, then we would lose these life-giving supports, and we would suffer. We take these instructions seriously, so ceremonies go on with their speeches of acknowledgment, songs, and dances. Our ceremonies are community affairs with people of all ages taking part. This we continue to do today.

A Jesuit priest of the 17th century noticed this, and he was frustrated by his inability to proselytize. "They have ceremonies for everything. They have a ceremony for getting up, a ceremony for going to sleep, a ceremony for birth, a ceremony for death, a ceremony for war, a ceremony for peace. Everywhere there is a confounded ceremony." Yes, it is true that we have ceremonies. In fact, as we speak there is a ceremony going on at Onondaga for planting. Tomorrow we will have a celebration for the spiritual beings that protect us. The next day there will be a ceremony for thanksgiving to the Creator, with our best clothes and our best minds, and the day after that a ceremony for the thundering voices we call our grandfathers, who bring the rain to give water to the people and the earth, yet another "confounded ceremony." And so it goes on, across the continent with reverence for life and life-giving forces: Hopi ceremonies, Navajo ceremonies, Cheyenne ceremonies, Lakota ceremonies, Seneca ceremonies. Ceremonies, ceremonies, those "confounded ceremonies."

Perhaps today we should have one grand ceremony to celebrate the survival of our religion or, as we call it, our "way of life." We have survived against the might of Christian proselytization. Perhaps we survive it because there are in our instructions things that may help to heal the earth and the minds of the people, a ceremony for peace, justice, and the health of good minds." §§§

Last year, 1993, marked the year that we finished the Draft Declaration on the Rights of Indigenous Peoples, at the United Nations in Geneva, Switzerland, after seventeen years of work. In the declaration you will find certain things that we have declared as essential to our human rights, and one of them is that we be designated as "peoples," and not as "populations" and not as "people," but as *peoples*. The point is important because for indigenous, or any, peoples, when you add the 's' to peoples, that means you are speaking of the Navajos and the Cheyennes, and you are speaking of *all* of the different peoples. But using a generic term like "people," which covers up our distinct identities, denies us our human rights. That's fundamental.

The Draft Declaration will go before the U.N. Sub-Commission this August, and it is going to go through what we call the meat grinder, where each nation-state will have a crack at it. We hope that the U.S. takes a strong position on that draft declaration, as we have written it, with those seventeen years of labor and trials. There are people who have died during the process. Even as recently as last fall, the Ashaninka representative from Peru who was at Geneva, a fine young man who worked very hard, was killed in a massacre of the Ashaninkas on the border of Peru and Brazil. That is how hard our people work. We suffered for that declaration, and we hope that all of you will support that declaration as we wrote it. §§§

Dr. Abdullahi An-Na'im, Executive Director
Human Rights Watch/Africa

To say that all religion—and for me as a Muslim, Islam—is a source of conflict and tension and violence and injustice, but also a cause for justice and peace, is to say the obvious. To say that as a Muslim I believe in Islam is to say very little, because it does not say what Islam is to me. I think the failures that we see are our failures, not the failures of "religion." What is important is the choices we make in our beliefs: not just the name, not the label Muslim or Christian or Jew, but the content of that belief, and not only as we articulate it, but also as we live it. We have to be absolutely certain that we are talking about human choices. I am not talking about divine directives. To understand the

Qur'an in its totality, and the lives Muslims have lived by it through the centuries, is what a human rights advocate with a Muslim perspective would try to do. §§§

A principled foreign policy is the only foreign policy that any country ought to have, especially one as powerful and influential as this country [the United States]. And to see that principle being played around with, sometimes subordinated to the expediencies of politics and power, is very discouraging. As a Muslim from Sudan, I know what's going on in Algeria. I know the same voices that are crying out for justice are being manipulated into confrontation, into violence. A principled foreign policy is not to go with labels, but to go with accountability to common standards of achievement. That is what the investigation of human rights has been and now is: commitment to shared standards of common achievement. That commitment has to persist across the board in every respect and not become a justification drawn on for expediency.

I come from a country where human rights are really in a terrible crisis. And there is the so-called tension between the secular and the religious, in that many of the human rights activists in our communities tend to shun religious discourse as a complication, as something which will concede authority, or authoritarianism, to violence and to narrow-mindedness. Therefore, they will have nothing to do with it.

I come also from a place where religion is raised as a beacon for justice and for social struggle for human dignity, but not necessarily seen in terms of human rights. And I think that is a dichotomy that we have tried to address in our paper [Universality vs. Relativism in Human Rights], and I think it is a dichotomy that must be reconciled.

Human rights advocates do not have a choice regarding religious discourse. Religious discourse is a reality for the vast majority of our constituencies, and if we do not take a stand on religious grounds in favor of human rights, that stand will be taken against human rights on the ground with which our own constituencies resonate the most. If you ask a Muslim to make a choice between Islam and human rights, I think the obvious answer will be, "I will stand by Islam." It's *only* when we can make Islam and human rights synonymous, in the thinking and feeling and motivation and action of our constituencies, that you can have a human rights world culture—globally, a human rights culture.

But if we maintain the tension, if we reject the dialogue between religion and human rights as attempting to bridge two irreconcilable world views, then I think it is our cause, the cause of human rights, that is likely to lose. For this reason, I plead that the choices, for those who are secularly inclined and for those who are religiously inclined, be made in the common cause of human rights. And I plead that foreign policy choices, regarding Algeria or regarding Sudan or regarding Rwanda, will be choices of principle and not choices of expediency. §§§

The Rev. Dr. Robert Drinan, S.J.
Professor of Law, Georgetown University

We come together on the feast of Pentecost. Bishop Moore said to me that it was not planned this way, but I think that it is providential. This morning the Pentecost liturgy reminded one and a half billion Christians once again of the source of human rights: Every single person is precious because every person is a tabernacle of the Holy Spirit. The Holy Spirit came in tongues of fire, and the apostles, who were uneducated, could speak in all tongues, and people heard. Centuries before the Christian Pentecost event, the God of Abraham, Isaac, and Jacob commanded us to see each person as precious. The book of Genesis states that each person is made in the image of God. Not only Judaism and Christianity, but all of the religions, talk about the value and uniqueness of every single human being. Each individual is a vessel that should be respected by the entire world, and that is the whole essence of human rights. The Holy Spirit becomes our advocate, our teacher, our inspiration within. St. Paul says that "the Holy Spirit groans to God for us." All religions share in the belief that somehow God dwells in us. It's not unique to the Jews or to the Christians; every single person has human rights that are indivisible and prescriptible, inalienable, and very sacred. These rights come to us from God. They are inseparable from our very being.

Christians have other reasons for their conviction that every soul is precious, and in the language of the law we call this preciousness "the human rights of the individual." By creation we become a member of the human family, and each person is selected by God to occupy a unique place in the human family. We also have knowledge from redemption that each individual is very precious to Christ himself. We suffer for everyone's humiliation when they are denied their human rights, but Christians also believe that Christ himself suffered in his thirty-three years as a true human being for every one of us. And if we had observed human rights more often, Christ literally would have suffered less during the agony in the garden.

We can recall what Governor John Winthrop, the first Governor of Massachusetts, said when Massachusetts was an overwhelmingly Protestant Christian community. John Winthrop said to the people of Massachusetts in 1640, "We must love one another with a pure heart fervently. We must delight in each other, make each other's condition our own, rejoice together, mourn together, and suffer together. We must be knit together as one." Tonight we can recall what St. Paul said: "Love is patient and kind, it does not pursue selfish advantage. Love is not jealous or conceited or proud. Love is the only thing that still stands when all else has fallen."

So we return to Pentecost and recall that St. Paul said, "All of us must make up for what is lacking in the sufferings of Christ." In that mysterious phrase we are reminded that "whatsoever we do for the least of Christ's brethren, we do unto him," and that Christianity is a Christocentric religion in which every individual is Christ himself. Christ redeemed that person by his exquisite suffering. If we deny the human rights of any individual, however obscure, anywhere around the world, we as Christians are saying, Yes, and denying the very rights and the sanctity of God. §§§

MESSAGE FROM BOUTROS BOUTROS-GHALI
Secretary-General of the United Nations

Read by Francesc Vendrell, Chief, Asia Unit
Office of the Secretary-General

I am pleased to send my best wishes to the participants of the Conference on Religion and Human Rights. Recognition of human rights is valued everywhere and for all people. The General Assembly of the United Nations in 1948 adopted and proclaimed the Universal Declaration of Human Rights. Since then the course of human rights has been consolidated in many ways: internationally, governmentally, by private organizations, and by courageous individuals in lonely and often desperate circumstances. At this time, with a new century in sight, when the further advancement of human rights should be at hand, there is no cause for complacency.

Voices are now heard which deny the very concept of universal human rights. Behind the cloak of exceptionalism and cultural difference, oppressive regimes are emboldened to disregard human rights. In many parts of the world, fears are rising that the international movement for human rights may be losing momentum. In these circumstances it is vitally important to return to fundamentals; for all religions, universal respect for human rights is part of the belief in the sanctity of creation.

As human beings sharing this earth, respect for human rights is, for us, a moral imperative, typified in religious admonitions to love and to deal justly with one's neighbors. For these reasons, your conference comes at the critical time. I commend you on your initiative and look forward to learning of the results of your deliberations.

FIRST PANEL OF WITNESSES: FORMER YUGOSLAVIA
Moderated by Jeri Laber, Executive Director
Human Rights Watch/Helsinki

Omar Sacirbey, First Secretary and Human Rights Advisor, Permanent Mission of the Republic of Bosnia-Herzegovina to the United Nations

The feeling of the government that I represent is that religion is one of the issues in the conflict in Bosnia-Herzegovina that has been very much misunderstood. As a result of that misunderstanding, there have been myths that in one form or another have staved off what we perceive as the actions necessary to put an end to the war.

I would like to address just two of these myths very briefly. The first is the myth of age-old ethnic hatred, that somehow the Bosnian Muslims and the Bosnian Serbs and the Bosnian Croats and others in the Republic of Bosnia-Herzegovina have had a history of thriving on the murder of one other; and because of these age-old ethnic hatreds, it is okay for the international community to step back, keep out, and let the slaughter continue. But the history of Bosnia-Herzegovina, if you look at it, will show that different ethnic groups and different religions have, in fact, co-existed peacefully and harmoniously for well over 500 years. One example is that when the Jews fled the Spanish Inquisition, they could have gone to Paris or to Geneva or to Frankfurt. Instead, they went from the westernmost ends of the continent to Sarajevo, knowing that under the Ottoman Empire their existence as a people, and their freedom to practice their religion and to preserve their identity, would not be compromised. They knew that there would be no harassment. You can look at the churches, synagogues, and mosques that have stood in Bosnia-Herzegovina for hundreds of years: together, in the same cities, on the same block, untouched until just a couple of years ago. So when you hear this myth of age-old ethnic hatred, whether it comes from U.S. or other officials, I ask that you keep in mind what I just said.

Secondly, there is the claim that this is an ethnic war, a religious war. In our view, although religion does play a very direct role in this conflict, it actually boils down to a political conflict. One view from Sarajevo is that the multi-ethnic, religiously plural existence, which has gone on for more than 500 years, should continue. And one view comes from the Belgrade regime headed by Slobodan Milosevic, who for his own political goals is having his surrogates in Bosnia fight for an ethnically cleansed Greater Serbia. So, when we look at the roots of conflict and at whether religion is a *root* in the conflict in Bosnia-Herzegovina, I would not describe religion as a root; I would actually describe it as a *tool* of conflict. §§§

The last point that I would like to make is about intervention. Some people say that we do not see action to intervene in Bosnia because the victims are Muslims. But, of course, others will say, "Well, what about Kuwait? What about Somalia?" I think we should point out that the question to be asked concerns whom the international community has taken action against since World War II. Specifically U.S. action was taken in Korea, in Vietnam, in Grenada, in Panama, and in Iraq: all peoples of either different colors or different religions. But when you find somebody of the same skin color and the same religion as yourself perpetrating genocide, as it is described by Human Rights Watch/Helsinki, the American Jewish Committee, the Armenian-American Congress, the International Court of Justice, and others, I think it is a lot more difficult to take action against this genocide. When we talk about the Serbian "ethnic cleansing" of non-Serbs, we talk about a government-instructed policy, and that's very important to note. I can quote one of the Mosevsky reports; it came out in November 1992: "Ethnic cleansing is the *objective* of the war here." It is not some kind of a by-product or consequence; it is the objective of the Serbian regime in Belgrade. "Ethnic cleansing" is a regrettable misnomer; this is a clear-cut case of genocide. §§§

Dr. Mitja Zagar, Wayne State University

Law and political science are my fields, and from these perspectives I am an advocate for and believer in human rights. I have been working especially on protection of the rights of minorities. I am an atheist, but as an atheist I have studied and I do still study, religions, beliefs, ceremonies, practices. I do respect them. I consider them a part of our culture and heritage. And I am a Slovenian, a former Yugoslav, and when I see the things going on in the parts of the country that once was my country, when I see the towns being destroyed where I used to walk, of course, I am emotionally affected. §§§

I see democracy as a process, not as a simple process, but as a complex and diverse process. Democracy does not mean the same thing for everybody. From the Western perspective, we tend to stress the importance of the individual and the individual alone. I would not want in any way to dismiss the importance of the individual, but I would like to draw your attention to various democracies in other parts of the world where the individual is not necessarily the basic principle of organization, where the local community makes decisions as a community. The ideology of individualism that actually is the basis of Western democracy is even more deeply rooted than democracy itself. It is an idea of competition, competition against others rather than cooperation with others. And this, of course, is reflected in different religions. At the same time we human beings have a need of community, of collective identity. We are social animals and need other people to function. In order to fulfill such needs, religions play a very important role all over the world. Religions are one of the tools or one of the means that enable us to develop the feeling of belonging.

I do see religions as providers of collective identity, but identity is not something that is constant and unchanging. I would argue for pluralism of identities. For me, the solution is not in denying them, but in recognizing them and promoting them—and in promoting also a new concept, a concept of cooperation which we can call the ideology of cooperation, or the religion of cooperation, if you want. It is something that is present in most religions already but has to be transformed into a practice and into concrete action. Is religion a problem or a solution? It can be both. It can be neither. It depends how it is presented and how it is utilized in practical, political circumstances. §§§

In the period after the Second World War, up to the 1990s, we did not have all these problems in our region. The problems occurred when democracy of the Western pluralist type was introduced. The problem is not that democracy as such was introduced, but that Western-type democracy requires certain political socialization, certain terms of reference which simply did not exist in the region. All of a sudden you had the freedom to form parties. What are you going to base these parties on? You have no political ideology, you have no political socialization, and you have no ideological background. In this context, political parties used the most logical way of mobilizing people: along ethnic lines. You had the collision of three ethnic political parties that are not based on different political ideologies but which have mobilized their supporters on an ethnic basis. As people were mobilized along ethnic lines, along religious lines to a certain degree, these conflicts became epic conflicts, and their ethnic dimensions grew.

I would like to tell a story that illustrates how this happens. A friend of mine in one of the northern Bosnian towns worked in the high school. He was a child from a mixed marriage: his father, a Croat; his mother, a Muslim. And he always felt he was loved. He was an atheist. He told me that one day he woke up, went to work, and found his Serbian colleagues had not come to the school. The next day they started to shell the city. And he said, "The day when the first shell exploded, they made me a Muslim." §§§

Julie Mertus, Esq., Counsel, Human Rights Watch/Helsinki

Just as women are visibly invisible in the discourse of nationalism, it appears to me that women are visibly invisible in the discourse of religion. I do not pretend to be an expert in what other people think. My own perspective is as a woman, as a human rights activist, as a lawyer, as the daughter of a man who came to this country for religious freedom, and as the daughter of a religious Slovak: that is my perspective. As has already been said, religion is not the root of the conflict here. Instead, religion, like ethnicity, with which it is carefully and artfully blended, is a tool for demonizing others. Religion is *used* by power groups in order to dominate in a given territory; it is not itself the cause of the conflict here.

I want to make a note on the notion of a collective memory, on historical memory, because there are several references in these papers [draft papers under discussion at the meeting] and elsewhere to the collective memory of the Serbian people, as if there is a single collective memory of Serbian people that promotes hatred towards Muslims, in particular, and a collective memory that promotes hatred toward Albanians.

I would like to suggest that this is not the collective memory of young people. Young people with whom I work in former Yugoslavia have a collective memory of listening to Beatles tunes and Muslim songs with mixed ethnic groups on the beach in Dubrovnik. I am stereotyping, of course, but that tends to be their collective memory. It is not a collective memory dating back to World War II or the Ottoman Empire. The so-called "collective memory" of the Serbian people is not the collective memory of urban dwellers either, for the most part. It is not the collective memory of intellectuals. And it is not the collective memory of women. The collective memory, as it is defined, uses, manipulates, and excludes women to some extent, so it is not women's collective memory either. In addition, it is not the collective memory of people in mixed marriages. So who has this collective memory? I suggest that since not many people do have a collective memory of hatred that can be automatically tapped, instead there has had to be a very artful, careful process in order to provoke, create, and exploit hatred based on religion and ethnicity. §§§

SECOND PANEL OF WITNESSES: THE MIDDLE EAST
Moderated by The Hon. Richard Murphy
Senior Fellow on the Middle East, Council on Foreign Relations

Eitan Felner, B'Tselem, Jerusalem

§§§ I would like to suggest a three-level taxonomy of human rights, specifying descending degrees of universality. This taxonomy may provide a weak version of cultural relativism, which I subscribe to, with a theoretical framework for determining which human rights are open to cultural interpretation, and to what extent.

The first level of the taxonomy is based on the inviolability of the human body. It provides the criteria for the determination of absolute, universal human rights which do not permit deviation on the basis of culture. An anthropology based on the idea expressed by the sociologist Bryan Turner that "human frailty is a universal feature of human existence" can provide the basis for claims about the universality of a core and very limited set of human rights, such as the right to life, particularly the prohibition of extrajudicial executions; the freedom from torture and other forms of cruel, inhuman, and degrading treatment; and some basic protection of economic rights, such as the right to food and the right to shelter.

This emerging anthropology claims that what is universally true about human beings, beyond cultural differences and regardless of historical contingencies, is neither being rational, as the vision of the Enlightenment made us believe, nor seeking transcendental meaning, as religious visions want us to believe. Our common humanity is rather more humble and mundane. As Umberto Eco said, "One could construct a whole ethic based on respect for the body and its functions, eating, drinking, pissing, defecating, sleeping, making love, talking, listening, and so on. To stop someone from sleeping at night, to force them to hang upside down, is a form of intolerable torture. Rape does not respect the body of someone else." I would suggest that even if we do not accept Eco's contention that a whole ethic could be constructed on the basis of respect for the body, it certainly provides justification for the universal validity of the core human rights norms.

The second level of this taxonomy does not stem from an anthropological/universal truth about the frailty of the human body, but rather from a practical, political necessity resulting from the historical condition of contemporary societies. It concerns a set of basic freedoms, such as freedom of speech, freedom of movement, and freedom of association.

Although this set of rights is necessary to protect individuals from the intolerance of those in power in different kinds of societies and existing under different historical and social conditions (as the fates of Socrates, Jesus, and Galileo, unfortunately, illustrate), their relevance has become particularly poignant for the protection of the individual in modern times. The conditions created by a variety of social and cultural processes of modernization—such as erosion of organic communities and the emergence of multicultural societies, urbanization, increasing individual mobility, mass communications, and, above all, the consolidation of the modern state—render the individual, as well as minority groups, particularly vulnerable without the protection of this set of rights.

In organic communities where individuals share an all-encompassing view of ethics, art, rituals, an historical narrative, and the same discourse, freedom of expression need not be, or at least needs less to be, a human right. However, without this organic unity, freedom of expression is necessarily a human right, as one of what Jack Donnelly called "the entitlements that ground particularly powerful claims against the state."

The third and last set of rights concerns more general questions of social and political institutions. They include many of the economic and social rights, such as the right to work and the right to education, as well as some of the political rights, such as the right to political participation. I would suggest that this set of rights allows for a greater degree of variation in interpretation. Depending on both cultural characteristics and social conditions, a scarcity of resources may require that various degrees of implementation be allowed, according to resources available. Nonetheless, it should be noted that even within this category, the legitimate range of variation has conceptual limits. As Donnelly illustrates, an election in which a people were allowed to choose an absolute dictator for life—"One man, one vote, once," as a West African quip puts it—in no way represents a defensible interpretation of the right to political participation.

I would like to sum up by saying that cultural differences cannot justify fundamental deviations from universal human rights standards. Culture can only be a limited source of interpretation with a comprehensive set of prima facie universal human rights.

Human rights set the boundaries of the intolerable. Their purpose is to protect the individual against the contingencies of political expediency, economic progress, and, not least, cultural relativism. §§§

Dr. Marnia Lazreg, Hunter College of the City University of New York

I am playing the role of the witness; I am witnessing within the context of Algeria. I do not address the Middle East as an expert. I am an advocate of the case study, because I do not think we know any one of these countries well enough to be able to make generalizations about all of them.

First the facts. Since 1992, when the second round of parliamentary elections was canceled, and the main opposition party, the Front of Islamic Salvation, was banned. More than 4,000 people died in Algeria in what is essentially a civil war, pitting government forces against not only the Front of Islamic Salvation, but also splinter groups, as well as the secularist vigilante group Free Young Algerians. In the first phase, violence was targeted at the state and its security apparatus—namely, the police, the military, and the national guard. In the second phase, violence was aimed at foreigners, including journalists. More recently, women and children have been added to the list of victims. My own seventy-six-year-old mother is in hiding after being threatened with death, and last March she received a phone call informing her that she would die by having her throat cut. As she tried to find out what she had done to merit such treatment, she was told that her fate had been decided. My niece, a professor of physics and chemistry, has lately been greeted in her classrooms with signs written in Arabic warning her that good Muslim women should not teach.

Violence against women merits special attention, because in its latest phase, it targets women *as* women. Indeed, at first some women were killed because they were relatives of men targeted by one terrorist group or another. For example, mothers and wives of police officers were killed in the same way that male relatives of those condemned to death were also killed in an apparent implementation of the notion of collective responsibility. However, in the last few weeks women have emerged as the main focus of violence. In mid-April signs appeared in the streets of Algiers warning women to wear the veil by a certain date, under penalty of death. This threat was carried out as a fourteen-year-old young woman and two university students lost their lives in Algiers because they failed to cover their heads. The story does not end here.

In retaliation, the secularist organization, Free Young Algerians, warned women against wearing their veils, and killed two who did. This organization actually vowed to kill thirty veiled women and "fundamentalist" men. Women of all ages have been killed in the last few months, the oldest being ninety-four. While some women were killed apparently because they engaged in activities such as fortune-telling (deemed un-Islamic), others were teachers, business-women, managers, hairdressers, and maids.

Rape, a crime that was not common in Algeria, now often precedes the murder of women. Thus a sixty-year-old woman was raped before being killed. Similarly, kidnapping women and children has become a widespread practice. The methods used in killing women include throat-slitting, decapitation, and, more rarely, shooting. Gathering witnesses is a *leitmotif* of violence. Murders usually take place in front of family members, as happened to a mother of five, who was decapitated in the presence of her children. Women also suffer from another form of violence that has not been reported by the press in this country—namely, physical maiming. A number of women going to work and coming back from errands have been slashed with razor blades or have had acid thrown at their faces.

Why is all of this happening? Is it religion that is the culprit? In my opinion, too much emphasis has been placed on religion, and on Islam, as the cause of so much of the social unrest that characterizes the contemporary Middle East, and especially Algeria. As a sociologist and a native of Algeria, I am convinced that the problem of social change—change from a predominantly agrarian society to an industrializing society, from the extended family to the conjugal family, to name only two aspects—is complex and cannot be solved by reducing it to a problem of religiosity.

This is because, first, there is no place in the Qur'an for justifying the murder of children, women, and men, some of whom were imams.

Second, historically, Algerians thrived on religious practices based on membership in a diversity of orders, the cult of saints, and a diffused tradition of occultism, especially among women. Puritanical attempts were made in the 1930s, when Algeria was still a colony of France, by upper middle-class socially conservative intellectuals to redirect the society toward a more scripturalist interpretation of religion, but this did not succeed, primarily because individuals thought of themselves as good Muslims already abiding by the five pillars of their religion. Algerians have also traditionally hung on to the belief that religion is a matter of individual conviction, not coercion.

Third, organized religion played a diminished role during the war of decolonization. The best example of how religious traditions inimical to women may be rendered inactive in political events is provided by the mass entry of women into the war between 1954 and 1962.

Fourth, the agenda presented by the religious movement bears little resemblance to the Qur'an. Indeed, the Front of Islamic Salvation advocated that women be paid to stay home, thus discouraging them from working. As you probably know, there is no reference in the Qur'an to women working.

What must be explained is why religious movements are able to use religion more successfully or less successfully to gain acceptance of their essentially political goals? The possible answer lies in the study of the socio-political, as well as the economic, contexts which give appeal to a simplified view of religious belief. For example, where unemployment is high among youths, advocating that women stay home because that is their God-ordained place may, indeed, become attractive. §§§

We must study the many factors in any given society that permit the interpretation or reinterpretation of religious values and traditions to fit mundane goals of religious movements. In other words, we must find out under what conditions religion becomes a tool of mobilization in a political struggle. Such an inquiry will reveal the paradoxical nature of religious movements which legitimize violence against fellow believers whom they ordinarily claim to protect, their definition of the enemy, and their understanding of what constitutes secularism.

In the Algerian case, the religious movement is not millenarian and is not necessarily anti-modern. It is culturally nationalistic and seeks to restructure the political, as well as the economical, spheres. Now, what does this have to do with women? Traditionally, women have been seen as symbols of cultural integrity, and there is a massive literature in the history of Algeria on how women have been used both by the French, during the colonial era, and by the Algerians to actually symbolize the culture. §§§

THIRD PANEL OF WITNESSES: SOUTH ASIA
Moderated by Sydney Jones
Executive Director, Human Rights Watch/Asia

Dr. Anand Mohan, Queens College of the City University of New York, and Secretary, Council of Hindu Temples of North America

It seems to me from a South Asian perspective that, by and large, neither the Hindu nor the Muslim society of India is fundamentalist in any of the senses mentioned in the second paper [draft paper prepared for the meeting]: for example, depending on textural literalism, insisting upon the inerrancy of doctrine, entertaining apocalyptic visions, or desiring the religious transformation of civil society. And although the Western media habitually refer to Hindu India and Muslim Pakistan, the governments of both countries set out originally, after their independence, to become essentially secular and continue to do so. This is not to say that religion does not intersect with politics in South Asia. §§§

Caution in speaking of so-called fundamentalist groups in the Middle East is advisable in judging the Hindu militants of the Bharatiya Janata Party, which cannot simply be dismissed as a band of thugs intent on wrecking one mosque after another. The BJP asserts that it is more devoted to the secular ideal than the Congress Party is. It claims even to have Muslims among its membership, and its definition is that of a secular, political party. What it maintains is that the Congress Party has done nothing but appeal to the most reactionary elements of the Muslim community. In effect, what the BJP is saying is that it wants to save the Muslims from the Congress Party, that the Party has cynically exploited the Muslims as vote banks, and that far from introducing a uniform civil code for a secular country, as promised by the Constitution, the ruling party has aided and abetted the suppression of the fundamental human rights of Muslim women in India. And by playing to the gallery of conniving Muslim politicians, Hindu India became, to its everlasting shame, the first country in the world to ban

Salman Rushdie's *Satanic Verses* and thereby to deprive the son of the soil not only of his fundamental rights, but also of his very reason for existence.

I personally think that it is only fair to admit that in the long and sordid story of the controversy surrounding the Babri Mosque at Ayodhya, it is not the Bharatiya Janata Party that appears in as bad a light as the executive branch of the government of India and the state government, which stand condemned as the culprit, and the judicial branch, which emerges as the villain of the piece.

§§§

Are all human rights complementary to each other? Or do some conflict with each other? Even allowing that there is no necessary conflict between different sets of human rights, can some of them claim priority over others? Is there a hierarchy of values that can help us arrange them in an acceptable order? Take, for instance, the ongoing agitation in India over the project for building a dam over the Narmada River. The environmentalists and the defenders of tribal culture are against the project, but the developmentalists and the modernists argue that millions of people will be better off with the blessings which the project will confer.

I now come to the troublesome question, Who has the right to talk about rights? Do religious leaders either in South Asia or from outside of the region have a right to raise the consciousness of over a billion people about their rights? Even their minimal survival rights? And bring about a revolution of rising expectations, which in no way they can hope to satisfy or fulfill? If there is no right without a remedy, what can religious leaders do materially and substantially to remedy the situation? The governments of South Asia are not any more perverse than the governments of the West. If they cannot, for obvious lack of resources, ensure even survival rights, there is bound to be political dissent accompanied by rising levels of resistance and militancy, which are likely to be suppressed by nervous and unstable governments faced with escalating levels of coercion and violence, compounded by a denial of primary uncontested political and fundamental rights. A vicious cycle would ensue, and would religious leaders then hold themselves morally responsible for their own creation?

Two ways out of this cycle suggest themselves to me: First, a greater reliance on the rhetoric of duties, because it is less adversarial and confrontational and because the internalization of the ethic of moral obligation, or *dharma*, is certainly conducive to the notion of reciprocity, even in the observance of rights. And secondly, the frank recognition by governments and peoples that some rights are simply not enforceable. This is done, for instance, in the Constitution of India, which distinguishes fundamental rights from directive principles of state policy. Whereas rights proper are considered enforceable in courts of law, the directive principles of state policy are not, but rather serve as guideposts for legislation and also lend themselves to the moral-political discourse that may lead to appropriate legislation. Such a distinction is also conducive to an understanding of the possibilities and limitations of human rights, thereby inducing a degree of becoming humility in all of us in the face of this awesome enterprise. §§§

Shazia Rafi, Director of Democracy and Development
Parliamentarians for Global Action

Whether religion is the *root* of conflict, or whether it is the *tool* that is used by other forces, I think is a moot point. For the last maybe 1,400 years, religion along the Hindu-Muslim divide, and also *within* both religions, has been a point of conflict in South Asia.

I think that there is a problem of integration that Muslims within South Asia feel because of their history. Islam came to India as part of a political invasion, and although it was spread by religious and Sufi scholars largely to the lower castes of the Indian caste system, its point of entry was that of a political and military invasion. This leaves the Muslims in a very uncomfortable position within South Asia, where they are either identified as the descendants of invaders or as converts from the lower castes. So there is very clearly a kind of integration problem on a socio-political level. This was exacerbated by colonialism.

The British government ruled with the policy of divide and rule, pitting Hindu against Muslim, which tended to worsen an already existing problem of integration. For most of the time the Muslims have been in India, they ruled as rulers, without completely integrating into the society. After that there was a period of struggle of about 200 years in which the divisions were deepened.

Independence itself came along religious lines. The leaders tried to reach out to the masses and started to use religious symbols because there was an existing problem between the communities. Unfortunately, there was no one of the vision of Nelson Mandela at the time who could have incorporated various communities' concerns. At that point in time, the majority was not able to accommodate the minority enough, and as a result the country was split along religious lines. Both the creation of Pakistan and the subsequent creation of Bangladesh came about because in both instances the political majority, whether defined religiously or ethnically, was not able to accommodate a political minority.

At the time of independence in Bangladesh, there was a mass religious genocide with Hindus, Sikhs, and Muslims killing each other. Close to a million people died; probably 11 million people were made homeless. So I think religion has very clearly been a strong point of conflict in South Asia. §§§

With regard to fundamentalism, I speak more on Pakistan since I am a bit more familiar with that country. In Pakistan the roots of fundamentalism have grown not as a spontaneous movement coming from within society, but as one that has been carefully nurtured, funded, and supported by a military dictatorship that has ruled the country for the greatest majority of its years. It was also fueled by the rise of power of the oil-rich kingdoms in the Middle East, which have funneled money to various religious fundamentalist institutions.

The military dictatorship itself provided in a certain sense an umbrella of support to these institutions, and it also deliberately used religion as a way of continuing its hold on society and as a way of continuing to deny the ways of democracy.

One sort of element that points to this analysis is that when we did have a return to democracy—in the last few years we have had three elections—the last election resulted in fundamentalist parties winning only 3 percent of the vote. However, their power within society goes beyond their power in terms of votes, because many of the religious fundamentalists' laws that were brought into our system were brought in by presidential ordinances. These ordinances are now on our books, and even popularly elected politicians in Parliament find they do not have the political courage to remove them, even though they have made such commitments in their political campaigns. §§§

I feel that "democracy" is a label that must include a respect for human rights. Otherwise, it can become the tyranny of the majority and can be used by politicians to incite religious and ethnic loyalties for their own political gain. That there are multi-party politics and frequent elections is no guarantee of democracy. And I think the institutions of democracy must be strengthened with the basic fundamentals of human rights, which include rights related to the judiciary, press, and Parliament. Religious organizations should be used in a positive sense by encouraging religious leaders to think positively about human rights, which should be part of the institutions that strengthen democracy. §§§

Lodi Gyari, Director, The International Campaign for Tibet

I would like to focus my comments on our experience as Tibetans with these issues that we are discussing this morning. I think most Tibetans have come to the conclusion that the problem in Tibet seems to be the attitude of the Chinese occupation forces toward the Tibetans, not just as an ethnic group, but also as a religious group: the Han chauvinistic attitude toward the Tibetan people, Tibetan culture, and Tibetan religion. That attitude definitely is one of the root causes of the problem that we have in Tibet. This not something that happened overnight. Unfortunately, the chauvinistic attitude toward the Tibetans by the Chinese is not limited just to Communist China, but because of the tradition, I think, that attitude was always there. With the introduction of the Communist ideology, the combination became a very, very powerful force.

Some years back when His Holiness the Dalai Lama came out with proposals for solving the conflict between Tibet and China, he did not emphasize the political or the legal aspects of the relationship. He rather dealt with the core: he insisted that the most important thing was that the Tibetans be allowed to preserve their own cultural, religious, and other identities; and if this was guaranteed by the Chinese government, he would be willing to think about trying to co-exist within a framework of one nation. This was a major concession with regard to the political status of Tibet. So the core problem as far as Tibetans are concerned is their culture and their religion.

The Tibetan culture and religion are almost inseparable. I think it would be very difficult to say that one aspect of Tibet is cultural and another is religious, because they are so interrelated. And this was also the case with the old Tibetan identity, if we trace it back, and even the Tibetan nationalism. Nationalism is a term that can be used in different ways. What I mean here is a Tibetan's commitment to his or her own identity. It is also very much related to strong religious beliefs. When the Chinese first started invading and occupying Tibet, the very term used by the Tibetan resistance movement was something like "the defenders of religion." In fact, the term that till this day is used to describe China's occupation is one that means "enemy of the faith of the Buddha." §§§

As for Tibetan Buddhism, even though in one way in our soul we are deeply religious, almost fanatically religious, at the same time we are not at all "fundamentalist." In fact, for being able to keep our struggle totally non-violent, the credit most definitely goes to our religion. I do not say that religion always plays a positive role; but I think that with regard to Tibet, it certainly played a very positive role. In fact, just last month when His Holiness was here on a visit to the United States, he shared an encounter that he had with a priest who had come from Tibet after spending nineteen years [imprisoned by the Chinese] in solitary confinement.

This monk met His Holiness for the first time, and while he was sharing his experiences, he broke down and said, "Your Holiness, at one point I really felt that I would fail. I would fail my faith." So His Holiness felt immediately, "This means that he almost gave up his vows; he almost renounced religion." And so His Holiness said, "Well, it's understandable." But the monk explained that what he meant was that during his nineteen years of solitary confinement, there was one period when he *almost* allowed himself to have some hatred for the Chinese authorities. And this is, I think, really remarkable: after so much suffering, he never ceased to be able to love.

So I think from our experience, Buddhism has been a very positive influence. It has kept people from becoming violent. We do have some young people, both in and outside of Tibet, who talk about resorting to violent methods. But if we look into their background, their training, we find that they never had the opportunity to come into closer contact with their religion and with their culture. Because of the Chinese occupation, they were brought up in isolation from their culture; or in exile they had a modern or so-called Western education and were taken away from their traditional training. §§§

FOURTH PANEL OF WITNESSES: THE UNITED STATES
Moderated by Preston Williams, Houghton Professor of Theology and Contemporary Change, Harvard Divinity School

Preston Williams

From the very beginning, religion has been involved in the African-American perspective on human rights. In the first encounter of the white and black peoples in about 1520, we were considered a people without law, religion, and civilization. There was segregation, enslavement, and dehumanization of African-Americans. We had to fight for status within the human family. Oddly, one of the ways in which the relationship was structured was in terms of religion, and we were given religion in many instances as a means of controlling us, to make sure that we became dutiful slaves on the plantations of the masters. The values which we cherish as the so-called Western values of equality and human rights were not extended to us. We had to engage in a fight for those values, and we used, in part, the religion which was given to us by the conquerors. We also used the values of the Enlightenment, which we learned from our life in the West. So although Thomas Jefferson could not see fit to include us as equal citizens, unless perhaps we were on an island somewhere in the Atlantic Ocean, we nonetheless took those values which Jefferson enunciated and which were also in religious faith. We built them into our own understanding of our person and into a resource base that we needed to establish our place on this particular continent. And over a period of time, we were successful.

There was then a three-way commerce between Africa, the Caribbean, and the United States, and one might add also England and Canada. As a consequence, African-Americans were instrumental in carrying these values from

America back to Africa, and in stimulating concerns for human rights and personhood in Africa, as well as in the United States. After the Treaty of Berlin, when Africa was carved up and given to the European powers, there was a cessation of this sort of commerce among blacks, and this sort of communication had to go underground. There were a series of organizations then established in the United States which fought on behalf of civil rights for people. From the beginning our conception of human rights included the cultural, the economic, the social, as well as the civil and political rights, because we were totally enslaved. It was not a part of us that was enslaved; all of us was enslaved. And we had to fight for the right to be free workers, as well as to fight for the right to vote. So we had a more holistic view of what was included in human rights than did a number of Americans.

The movements which later developed, such as the NAACP, principally fought for liberal democratic traditions. The religious groups remain aligned with the NAACP, supplying the base of membership and much of the leadership for that particular organization. You also had religious components in the Garvey Movement, and then the Father Divine Movement, which were, in a way, movements oriented toward the achievement of civil rights. Most recently, of course, you have had the civil rights movement, and the leadership of Martin Luther King, Jr. Here again, you had a voluntary association which was much influenced by the churches, their leaders, and their membership fighting for human rights. You also had the influence of these religious groups on secular groups. So if one speaks of groups like SNCC, the Black Panthers, the Black Muslims, one is talking about groups which also had a religious thrust to them. That, I think, comes from the dominant history of the involvement of religious forces and groups and the fight for equality of African-Americans here in the States.

In more recent days, I think, one would point to the presence of pluralism in respect to both religion and culture among African-Americans. After World War II and de-colonization, one could resume the movements of people from Africa and the African Caribbean into America more easily than before. As you know, it was during this period that we ceased to have exclusionary [immigration] policies toward people from Asia and other parts of the world, and America then became a haven for people who were non-white, as well as a haven for whites. And in this period a greater diversity has come into the African-American community, with a number of cultures and sub-cultures, not only of the Christian-Protestant religion, but also large numbers of Roman Catholics, as well as peoples from African religious traditions. There are various versions of Islamic community, and blacks have been in the Islamic community here for a long period of time, not just in this latter period.

Tonya Frichner, Esq., Snite Clan, Onondaga Nation
President, American Indian Law Alliance

For over five centuries, relations with American Indian nations have been one of the darkest stains on American history. From the earliest encounter of Indians and European peoples, the relationship has been shaped by European culture and European cultural antagonisms with a significant religious dimension.

Early settler societies arrived in North America convinced of their cultural and moral superiority. Territorial consolidation was achieved through forced dispossession and genocidal practices that were justified with Biblical citations. Christian missionary activities were initiated in vulnerable Indian societies. The missionary imperative was a form of aggressive universalism explicitly denying the authenticity of the Indian culture and spiritual identity. Religious conversion invariably resulted in community fragmentation and erosion of both cultural coherence and traditional leadership structures, rendering Indian societies increasingly subject to external influence and control.

After the Civil War, Christianity played a direct role in territorial expansion and the colonial process. During the Grant Administration, Indian nations in the West were confined to reserved areas within their ancestral territories, initially under military control. The administration of the reservations was soon distributed to Protestant denominations; and the Catholic Church, which established Indian paramilitary police forces under its direct control, was authorized by Congress to replace the military.

The police enforced a code of Indian offenses which was designed by the government to suppress traditional practices, facilitate cultural assimilation, and weaken resistance to political domination. The code outlawed "heathen" practices, essentially outlawing Indian religious and inheritance practices. The Sun Dance and other ritual dances were forbidden, along with medicine activities and the Dead Feast, which was condemned as a disincentive to capital accumulation. The period of missionary administration lasted for a decade, but Christian denominations continued to press for and participate in policies of cultural assimilation. Missionaries ran many of the boarding schools in which Indian children were separated from their communities and from the older generations, and children were forced to suppress their languages, spiritual traditions, and cultural identities.

Additionally, Christian reform movements, joined by Western land interests, successfully advocated breaking up communal territories into small, private parcels of land. Reformers viewed the breaking up of the tribal mass—in other words severing the communal bonds that formed the core of the Indian identity—as necessary to facilitate a civilizing mission. Indeed, in 1903 the Supreme Court, in upholding the power of Congress to enforce the allotment of Indian land and seizure of the surplus, could say without irony that it presumed that the government, and I quote, "would be governed by such considerations of justice as would control the Christian people in their treatment of an ignorant and dependent race." Previously forbidden traditional ceremonies, such as the Sun Dance, were ultimately revived after the Second World War. During the cultural revitalization of the 1960s and 1970s, ceremonies were performed extensively without hindrance throughout Indian country. But official tolerance did not cross over to legal recognition until enactment of the American Indian Religious Freedom Act in 1978. This recognition was somewhat symbolic, however. Although Congress affirmed the inherent right of freedom to believe in, express, and exercise traditional religions, the Act provided no basis for legal protection of those rights beyond the First Amendment. Nevertheless, the long era of direct suppression was brought to a formal close. Today's spiritual traditions thrive in Native societies.

Howard Berman, Esq., California Western School of Law

Despite changes of unquestioned importance, Indian religious rights have not been fully realized. The historical legacy of dispossession and cultural conflict continues to impact vital spiritual traditions in situations where Indian religions come into contact and contention with the interests of the dominant society. For example, in many cases sacred sites and burial grounds located within ancestral territories now have the status of private or public lands. Preserving the integrity of these sites, assuring access for ceremonial purposes, and maintaining secrecy and privacy for communal and personal worship have proven difficult.

Sacred sites are natural world centers of spiritual power. Maintaining the integrity of places of spiritual significance requires preservation of their eco-logical character. Alterations of the landscape or resource extraction result in desecration and weakening of the spiritual connection. Although public and private land use decisions are not intended to suppress Indian religions, the ef-fect of these activities is equally devastating.

Indian peoples have also been dispossessed of sacred and ceremonial objects that are integral to cultural and spiritual traditions but are now held in museums and private collections. Part of the communal patrimony of the whole people, these objects were often obtained through purchase or fraud from individuals with custodial responsibility for their preservation. Some of these objects must be spiritually tended, requiring active participation in specific ceremonies. Others are necessary for the proper performance of ritual practice. Still others, such as the Iroquois wampum belts, contain the symbolic cohesion of the nation. In certain instances mere display to persons not authorized to see or touch them constitutes a desecration. Museums all over the world also hold Indian ancestral remains that were exhumed for scientific study and exhibition, a phenomenon that is tolerated only when the remains are from indigenous peoples.

Indian religious rights have also been violated by laws and regulations of general application that were drafted without regard for their impact on spiritual practices. In a number of states, ceremonial use of peyote and other psychotropic plants has resulted in criminal prosecutions under the general penal laws. Even were such prosecutions not actively pursued, the criminalizing of the central sacrament of the Native American Church has had a chilling effect on practitioners. Indian persons have also been prosecuted under conservation laws for acquisition of eagle feathers and for other acquisitions from protected species that are necessary for ceremonies and healing.

Additionally, federal and state prison regulations have prevented Indian inmates from having access to spiritual leaders at ceremonies, wearing long hair, and possessing medicine bundles immune from institutional observation. Although mainstream religious practices have been accommodated in prison settings, American Indian spirituality has not received similar recognition or respect. Consequently, Indian prisoners are more completely cut off than others from their spiritual and cultural communities.

Efforts to gain constitutional protection for these rights under the free exercise of a religion clause of the First Amendment generally have been rejected by the courts. Litigation seeking to secure the integrity of sacred sites on public land has been notably unsuccessful. For several decades federal courts balanced claims asserting that the free exercise of non-mainstream religion was impeded by federal or state action of general application, on one hand, with notions of compelling governmental interest.

In most cases, state governments were directed to reconcile their policies with the needs of religious practice, unless issues of national security or public order were involved and no feasible alternatives were available. In Indian sacred sites cases, however, the courts applied a considerably lower threshold, finding that government economic development projects on public lands outweighed the rights of Indian nations to preserve the environmental integrity of areas of spiritual significance.

These cases are examples of cultural and even cosmological conflict. The cultural expectations and religious mindset of the dominant society is reflected in the inability of the judiciary to accord full recognition and respect to the inseparable connection between Indian religions and the natural world. Christianity, in particular, sharply distinguished spirit from matter. In the words of the philosopher Alan Watts, "There is a deep and extraordinary incompatibility between the atmosphere of Christianity and the atmosphere of the natural world." The Christian cosmology is otherworldly, with an emphasis on transcendence of material limitations. Although sacred sites, such as the Wailing Wall, the Dome of the Rock, and Calvary, are certainly known in the majority religions, these spiritual places are regarded as consecrated by ritual and worship, rather than as possessing inherent sacred power of their own.

American Indian spirituality represents an entirely different way of being in the world. As Oren Lyons so eloquently described last night [at the opening of the meeting], Indian religions celebrate the Creation. Indian peoples inhabit a spiritualized universe in which the animate and inanimate aspects of the natural world resonate with the integrity of their own spirit. Human beings are part of a community of life. Plants and animals that sustain human societies are accorded the same respect as peoples. Although all things in the natural world are imbued with spirit, certain places in the landscape have a particularly significant sacred power. Traditional Indian societies carry a responsibility to follow their original teachings and to perform a ceremonial cycle necessary for maintaining spiritual harmony in the world.

Now, in the absence of effective judicial protection of these spiritual rights, an effort has been made in Congress to gain some legislative recognition and protection, with mixed results. There is currently a bill pending that would address some of the issues that I have outlined: protection of sacred sites—I should say *partial* protection of sacred sites—some recognition of non-traditional practices in relation to peyote, the status of Indian prisoners, and the status of protected species that are necessary for Indian worship. That initiative has not gone very far today.

The most extensive, at least in principle, set of standards recognizing the validity of indigenous spiritual practices, including American Indian religious rites, is emerging within the United Nations human rights system in the form of a Draft Declaration on the Rights of Indigenous Peoples. The text of that declaration has been initially finalized, although it now passes into the political organs of the United Nations, which are dominated by governments. To date it has been drafted in a cooperative process involving an expert body in the U.N., with some guidance from indigenous peoples and some involvement from a few interested governments as well.

As it passes into the more political realm of the United Nations, there is a very realistic possibility that it is going to be watered down and perhaps even eviscerated. One of the troubling aspects of this political process, for me—and I should say, for us—is that within the past year the U.S. State Department seems to be solidifying a position that is critical and takes an oppositional stance to some of the most important conceptual aspects of the declaration. And we would certainly urge those of you who have an interest in advancing standards and understanding for the rights of indigenous peoples, not only in the United States, but also in other countries, to let the State Department know that the U.S. position is not consistent with a full recognition of human rights in the world.§§§

The name John Winthrop came up last night when Robert Drinan gave his presentation. He quoted an aspirational statement by the good governor. Unfortunately, the practices of the New England Puritans were not so aspirational in relation to the rights of the American Indian nations that neighbored those settler societies. In fact, on the boat over [to New England], Winthrop wrote in his journal celebrating the fact that the Massachusetts Bay area was what he termed in Latin *vacuum domicilium*—the house is empty, the land is empty—and praising his God for sending disease to New England to remove the Indian nations that inhabited precisely that area. Also during his tenure as governor in Massachusetts Bay, the first genocidal military expeditions were launched against Indian nations in New England. I should also add in a general sense that the laws of Massachusetts Bay prescribed the death penalty for any Roman Catholic or Quaker who set foot on those shores. §§§

Considering the diversity of those attending, there was a high degree of consensus among the participants in the May meeting as to what the Project on Religion and Human Rights should do next. The small working groups of the conference reported in writing after its conclusion, prioritizing each group's concerns and proposing future programs. The Project has developed a plan for the next phase of work from these recommendations and after further consultation with experts in relevant areas. While work in a variety of modes is envisioned, the planned programs have an organic unity which emerges from the interconnection of the central questions in religion and human rights, an interconnection which we hope the first year's study process has demonstrated.

There was virtually unanimous agreement at the conference that the perspectives of women and indigenous peoples had been neglected in the first drafts of the four papers. In response to these omissions, the papers published in this volume have been extensively revised. The Project also has commissioned separate studies on these two subjects, and it is planning a conference on Women, Religion, and Human Rights.

Participants called for the collection and dissemination of basic information on religion and human rights, and the Project will fill this need with a directory of individuals and groups working in this area, a compilation of modern human rights documents, and further development of information resources. The

Project was also charged at the May meeting with the promotion of human rights education appropriate for the general membership of religious communities, clergy, and lay leaders. Our goal is to increase knowledge of human rights and to foster the values which uphold them. The Project will create a versatile "toolbox" of curricula for this purpose. A closely related task will be to publish a sourcebook of scriptural and traditional texts from each religious tradition which support and clarify that tradition's relation to human rights. Studies on particular topics will be continued on an ad hoc basis. Finally, special attention will be given to interfaith dialogue as an essential element of this overall program.

Editors' Concluding Reflections

The work of the Project on Religion and Human Rights is just beginning, a fact evident from the tentative character of the preceding papers, as well as their calls for further research and dialogue. Thus, to write concluding reflections on the inquiries initiated by these papers and by discussions at the Project's May 1994 meeting may be somewhat premature and even misleading. Religious traditions and the activities associated with human rights advocacy have a dynamic and even experimental character. Similarly, the intersection between religion and human rights, which the Project seeks to encourage and expand, may be expected to yield further activity and development. Indeed, the unanimous conclusion reached by all participants in the Project, including those attending its May meeting, is this: There is much to be done; the Project has so far only barely scratched the surface; and continuation of this work is essential if we hope to see religions contribute further to the strengthening and expansion of human rights in the modern world.

Such continuation, of course, needs direction, and although some guidance is provided by our papers, it seems important to highlight certain themes and ongoing issues that may be crucial for future work in the area of religion and human rights. The work reflected in this volume raises a number of issues, some of which may be easier to address than other more recalcitrant ones, but all of which need to be acknowledged. In what follows we will attempt to sketch the contours of the most salient issues by offering four sets of reflections concerning, respectively, religion and violence, religion as a resource for peace and human rights, the status of human rights vis-a-vis religious traditions, and the politics of recognizing oppressed groups.

RELIGION AND VIOLENCE

Our first set of reflections, not surprisingly, has to do with the relationship between religion and violence and, most particularly, the phenomenon of religious violence—that is, violence committed in name of religion. All of the Project's participants have been deeply concerned about the apparent increase of instances of intergroup conflict in which one or more of the contending parties appeals to religion as a way of justifying, or at least excusing, violent activities. At their worst, such conflicts associate religion with genocide or something very close to it—e.g., in Bosnia. Similarly heinous are the many cases of violence against women—e.g., systematic rape undertaken for reasons of ethno-religious cleansing. And even when the level of explicit violence is comparatively low— as, for example, in the United States—the rhetoric of some groups clearly projects implicit justifications of violence against those identified as, for example, "anti-God," "anti-Christ," "unbelievers," and "secularists." Whether one speaks of the rise of "fundamentalism" or prefers terms such as "religious militancy," the growth of religious violence is a major theme of the papers here, as well as a major concern voiced at the May meeting.

Many participants in our discussions conveyed a special concern to disassociate religion from violence. Sometimes this concern was framed in terms of a distinction between "true" (or authentic) religion, which was perceived to seek only peace, and "false" religion, which was perceived as more militant. At other times, the disassociation was effected by a critique of political leaders or elites who for self-interested ends appear to use religious values and imagery in cynically manipulating the allegiances and beliefs of the people and communitites over which they seek to maintain control—for example, in former Yugoslavia, Sri Lanka, or Algeria. Rightly understood, many participants insisted, religions are a source of peace and cooperation, not of violence and war, and should not be blamed for the tragic consequences resulting from the "bad faith" of powerful political leaders and elites.

Other participants in our discussions, however, appeared to be suspicious of claims about the intrinsic peaceful orientation of religious traditions, suggesting that the relationship between religion and violence is much more ambiguous and complex, both in historical cases (e.g., the conquest of indigenous peoples and their territories) and in contemporary contexts. Such suspicion is supported by the argument of this first paper that religion should be understood as one of several roots of conflict and violence. In particular, religious traditions integrate persons into identifiable groups and thereby differentiate these groups from other groups. This creates a psychosocial dynamic between "in" group and "out" group that, together with other factors, may help fuel intergroup conflict.

Similarly, the paper on fundamentalism depicts certain groups as attempting to be faithful to certain versions of their respective religious traditions. Such versions are necessarily partial and thus generate "in" groups that can contrast strongly not only with other versions and groups within the same traditions, but also with groups outside these traditions. As one of our consultants put it, no matter how much one wishes to say that "true Orthodoxy" or "true Catholicism" or "true Islam" would not sanction the well-publicized atrocities in the Bosnian war, and no matter how much truth there is in the thesis that certain leaders in that area are cynical political manipulators of religious symbols, one must still ask what makes such manipulations toward violence not only possible but also plausible to their respective peoples and communities.

For those who study the history of religious traditions, there is ample evidence that religion *is* a root of conflict, just as there is ample evidence of religion being used as a tool by cynical political leaders. There is also ample evidence that religion has contributed to peaceful avoidance and resolution of conflict.[1] Such diverse evidence suggests the need for careful case-by-case analysis of how religion functions differently in particular settings, whether for violence or for peace. When it comes to violence in general, it is worth pondering the observation of a contemporary military historian that as difficult as it may be for many to accept, there are persons and groups who consider violence, even in its most abominable and seemingly unjustifiable forms, as the most compelling and desirable alternative available to them.[2] This stark judgment about the human condition rings true, and it comports with the important observation that religion is simultaneously one of the most constructive *and* one of the most destructive forces in human life. The problem for all of us is to identify those factors that support its constructive development, while at the same time mitigating its destructive potential: this cannot be done if we bury our heads in the sand and pretend that religion is only inherently peaceful and constructive.

RELIGION AS RESOURCE FOR PEACE AND HUMAN RIGHTS

Many, if not most, of the participants in the Project's discussions wanted to affirm that the connection between religion and violence is not the whole story. This theme too is a major concern of this collection's papers, inasmuch as they

---

[1] See, for example, the case studies in Douglas Johnston and Cynthia Sampson, eds., *Religion, The Missing Dimension of Statecraft* (New York: Oxford University Press, 1994).

[2] Martin van Creveld, *The Transformation of War* (New York: Free Press, 1991).

conclude with hopes for, respectively, revisioning religious narratives, deepening and extending religious education, promoting internal and cross-traditional dialogues, and encouraging tradition-oriented monitoring activities. Perhaps the most poignant expression of such hopes came during the May meeting when a representative of the Jain tradition began to circulate a petition calling on all people to recognize the sanctity of human life and stipulating that "killing in the name of God is an abomination." Underlying these various expressions is a concern to affirm the positive role of religion in human life. For those who identify with a particular religious tradition, it is important to make public affirmations of the resources of their tradition for bettering personal and social life. Beyond this, there are elements in virtually all religious traditions that support peace, tolerance, freedom of conscience, dignity and equality of persons, and social justice. Needless to say, these are precisely the moral values that lie behind human rights declarations, covenants, and conventions. Indeed, as indicated by the fourth paper, in many cases the moral teachings of religious traditions go further in affirming and supporting such values than do contemporary statements of human rights. Moreover, although religions, in fact, generate distinctions between "in" group and "out" group, most of them also normatively project a universalism that incorporates all persons within one large extended family.

There is no reason to doubt these claims on behalf of religious traditions, for it is hard to deny that religious teachings have been a significant factor in the consciousness and life of some of the people most active in pursuing the goals identified with human rights: for example, U Thant, Dag Hammarskjold, Eleanor Roosevelt, Muhammad Zafrullah Khan, Martin Luther King, Jr., Thich Nhat Hanh, and the Dalai Lama, to name but a few prominent figures. These people, and the resources identified in this volume, remind us that religion has been an important force in fostering concern for human rights. They also provide evidence that such contributions can be expected to continue. Yet there is a special import in the attempt to identify at the present time the positive resources of religion for human rights. This is so for several reasons.

To begin with, such attempts remind believers and nonbelievers alike that religious sentiment and commitment are not just the prerogative of those who are currently labeled "fundamentalists" or "religious militants." As we have seen, "fundamentalist" appropriations of religious traditions do express a possible, although partial, understanding of one or another tradition. But they ought not to be granted sole proprietary rights to interpreting their traditions. In assessing the relations between religious traditions and human rights, perspective is essential. Contemporary religious militancy reflects the power of particular historical, social, and political contexts, even as it reflects the power of religious symbols.

If one can err in the direction of explaining away fundamentalism as a function of political interests, one can also err in the direction of accepting fundamentalist claims at face value. Attempts to identify correlations between religious traditions and human rights thus have special contemporary significance insofar as both believers and nonbelievers need to hear of the ways in which religious traditions have served and continue to serve as forces for building peace, justice, and tolerance in human affairs.

A second rationale for emphasizing religion's positive resources for human rights rests on the simple fact that religion and religious traditions are not going to disappear. In addition to meeting spiritual concerns, religion addresses fundamental psychological and social needs related to personal and group identity. For the vast majority of human beings, in the latter regard, the power of religion is unsurpassed. Such a correlation between religion and identity helps to explain the importance of an observation made by every student of the history of religions: Religious traditions rarely (if ever) pass away, but rather adapt again and again to new and changing situations. Or perhaps more accurately phrased, adherents of religious traditions invariably find ways to make them relevant to the continually changing conditions in which the social and psychological needs of integration and differentiation make themselves felt. The contemporary identification of the constructive resources of religion for human rights concerns is, therefore, important in encouraging the adaptation of historic traditions to a world context that sorely needs ways to find the means to safeguard the dignity and security of human beings.

Finally, the effort to identify the positive resources of religion for human rights is important insofar as it fosters dialogues between adherents of the same and different traditions, and especially between those who are not fundamentalist and those who are. In the latter regard, a number of participants made the point that in the future it is necessary to involve advocates of fundamentalist interpretations of religious traditions in the work of the Project. In the setting of the conference, no one knew quite what to do with this suggestion, particularly since one of the factors motivating concerns about the relationship between religious traditions and the human rights community was the behavior of militant religious groups, at least some of which must be judged as adverse to human rights. As the work on the volume's papers continued, however, it became increasingly important to recognize how many militant or fundamentalist groups do, in fact, function to safeguard and advance interests clearly consonant with current understandings of human rights—for example, affirmations of the value of human life and the provision of social services to peoples whose governments seem unable or unwilling to satisfy basic material needs. Furthermore, we ourselves must be careful not to cast fundamentalism as a radically alien "other," particularly since much in this phenomenon resonates with non-fundamentalists as well—e.g., worries about technology, materialism, radical individualism, and erosion of family and community values. Thus, it appears that there may be grounds for dialogue between fundamentalist and non-fundamentalist interpretations of religious and moral values within and among discrete traditions, and even perhaps between fundamentalists and human rights advocates.

None of the preceding analysis should be taken to suggest that there are not difficult philosophical and political issues involved in identifying the positive resources of religions for human rights. At the philosophical level, there are, for example, issues of how to interpret and appropriate elements of particular traditions. Even simple collections of passages from basic scriptures can be difficult. After all, texts seemingly concerned with peace and tolerance are often presented in connection with struggles, even violent ones, for justice on the part of a particular community. Who is to say definitively that the "meaning" of the texts in question has to do with values consonant with human rights, or not? Moreover, we need to be wary of focusing exclusive attention on textually-derived, idealized moral visions and ignoring the concrete evolution of traditions. Problems of interpretation become even more complex when we deal with long-standing social and religious practices which have been formed and continuously changed in subtle and complex ways. And, even if these problems can be constructively managed, there remains the issue of internal disagreement among members of religious communities. This issue suggests others at a more political level: for example, questions about the authority of religious organizations and institutions to speak for particular traditions, as well as problems in the relations between religious organizations and the institutions of established governments. These are familiar issues to anyone involved in human rights advocacy and will need to be considered in any future work aimed at fostering connections between religious traditions and human rights. While we cannot here resolve any of these problems, we can perhaps remove at least one obstacle to exploring such connections—namely, the fear that human rights simply represent a Western moral ideology intended to supplant the moral perspectives of the diverse religious traditions.

HUMAN RIGHTS IN RELATION TO RELIGIOUS TRADITIONS

While all the participants in the Project's conference expressed support for the concerns embedded in human rights documents such as the Universal Declaration of Human Rights, some suggested a concern that leads to this third set of reflections. What is the relationship between the universal claims of human rights as a kind of "minimal morality" and the more particular, usually richer and more extensive moralities advanced by religious traditions?[1] To a certain extent, this concern echoes issues of universality and relativism discussed in the third paper of this collection. Yet there are other dimensions to the concern as well. For example, some participants worried that a typical liberal understanding of human rights, conceived as a set of core moral principles constituting a foundation for moral judgments about behavior in very diverse cultural settings, means that human rights are implicitly imperialistic. Some interpreters hold that the core morality of human rights ought to be everyone's morality. Does this position not imply the end, or at least irrelevance, of the particular religious and moral traditions that have emerged in the context of various cultures? To put the question more bluntly, do advocates of human rights mean to replace existing religious traditions with some sort of "new faith"?

Moreover, there are questions about the metaphysical and epistemological assumptions associated with the promotion of human rights as a "foundation" for universal moral judgments.[2] These specifically philosophical questions are matters of hot debate. If, as many critics assert, claims about human rights are based on problematic conceptions of human nature and moral knowledge, then adherents of religious traditions may wonder whether they are being asked to accept ideas that are no longer regarded as valid. At the very least, such people may ask for a clearer explication and defense of the core principles of human rights than often seems available.

Without addressing all of the philosophical issues raised at this point, our Project's papers and conference discussions might be taken to suggest a more pragmatic approach to the relationship between specific human rights norms and particular religious traditions. Such an approach starts with the facts of pluralism and religious-moral particularity and finds that in situations of crisis, peoples of quite different traditions are able to acknowledge their mutual respect for certain basic or "minimalist" values. The Universal Declaration, for example, was the historical product of a very particular crisis brought about by genocide and brutal abuses of rights occurring during the Second World War. In the face of this

---

[1] These reflections are inspired, in part, by Michael Walzer, "Moral Minimalism," in his *Thick and Thin: Moral Argument at Home and Abroad* (Notre Dame: University of Notre Dame Press, 1994), pp. 1-19; originally published in William Shea and Antonio Spadafora, eds., *From the Twilight of Probability: Ethics and Politics* (Canton, MA: Science History Publications, 1992). We are much indebted to this illuminating article.
[2] For some provocative discussions of these questions, see, e.g., Gene Outka and John P. Reeder, Jr., eds., *Prospects for a Common Morality* (Princeton: Princeton University Press, 1993), especially the contributions of Alan Gewirth, David Little, John Reeder, Jeffrey Stout, and Richard Rorty.

crisis, representatives of a number of cultural traditions were able to recognize their mutual agreement on the judgment that such acts were antithetical to each and to all of their traditions. Similarly, the subsequent human rights Covenants of the 1960s were born from the mutual recognition that the oppression and material disadvantage suffered by peoples in developing countries were incompatible with moral sensibilities reiterated in a number of particular religious and moral traditions. A similar process led to the 1981 Convention on protection of women's human rights, and more recently to the United Nation's 1993 Draft Declaration on the Rights of Indigenous Peoples. The point is that far from preempting or replacing the rich moral teachings embedded in various cultural traditions, specific expressions of human rights concern have arisen from the mutual recognition by adherents of these traditions that they have a shared interest in the protection of certain values. Brutality, tyranny, starvation, displacement, and the like are recognized by adherents of all traditions as their common enemy. This recognition implies that despite evidence of cultural difference, many (if not all) traditions do, in fact, share important substantive moral values. At least in certain critical moments, participants in otherwise diverse traditions find that they have a shared set of aspirations, as well as a shared capacity to suffer at the hands of those who violate the dignity of human beings.

For pragmatic purposes, then, participants in religious communities and in the community of those concerned for human rights might consider specific expressions of human rights as products of successive recognitions by diverse peoples of a set of values embraced by their own distinctive cultural traditions. No one cultural tradition is the sole source of human rights concerns. Human rights are, from this point of view, the expression of a set of important overlapping moral expectations to which different cultures hold themselves and others accountable.[1] Moreover, since there is as yet no end to the suffering human beings impose on each other, we can expect to see additional moments of recognition, the addition of new rights to those already specified, and the emergence of new types of human rights emphases. Looming large on the current horizon are, for example, acknowledgements of the cultural rights of indigenous peoples and, partially as a result, the furtherance of rights claims aimed at the protection and preservation of the natural environment so highly valued by the traditions of many indigenous peoples.

---

[1] See Walzer, "Moral Minimalism," especially pp. 17-18.

POLITICS OF RECOGNIZING OPPRESSED GROUPS

One of the most striking features of the Project's conference was the demand for greater attention to the human rights of women and of indigenous peoples. This demand reflects one of the most consistent and far-reaching developments of our time: pressure to recognize the existence and validity of human diversity, particularly as expressed in the concerns of heretofore neglected or excluded groups and traditions. This development has a religious form, especially in the context of various ecumenical bodies and interfaith activities. It also has a human rights form, expressed, for example, in the long-standing project to develop a Declaration on the Rights of Indigenous Peoples and in the United Nations observance in 1993 of the Year of Indigenous Peoples. Comparable developments regarding women's human rights include, for example, the Convention on the Elimination of all Forms of Discrimination Against Women, which came into force in 1981, as well as more recent activities by nongovernmental organizations involving collaborations of women from diverse cultures and traditions. The Project's post-conference plans moved first in the direction of remedying pertinent deficiencies in this volume's papers, then to commissioning two entirely new papers. The papers on women's human rights and on the rights of indigenous peoples will be published in the near future. We are reminded here of the third paper's emphatic observation that the voices of the oppressed are the most important in dialogues about human rights.

A number of issues call for further activities, both political and reflective. The knottiest of these might be formulated as follows: To what extent can the current political and philosophical structures of international human rights be reconciled with the just demands of women and indigenous peoples? With respect to women's human rights, the issues are often framed in terms of claims about the universality of human rights versus claims about the particularity of cultural norms and practices. As the third paper shows, this formulation of the problem may be usefully addressed by paying attention to the variety of actors involved in human rights discourse, as well as by taking care to distinguish the diverse types of claims such actors make. Apparent contradictions between particular cultural norms and judgments on human rights issues are often not so clear when one unmasks the power interests (e.g., patriarchy) served by claims of cultural particularity and relativism. Furthermore, even where differences are real, there are possibilities for significant reflection and dialogue based on distinctions between negotiable and non-negotiable rights.

With respect to the claims of indigenous peoples, resolutions may be more difficult to achieve. In particular, the presuppositions of many of the institutions and instruments of human rights—e.g., concerning state sovereignty and concerning individuals as the primary focus of rights protections—appear to be in some tension with important aspects of indigenous experiences and world views. In political terms, there is much work to be done in responding, for example, to indigenous peoples' claims to sovereignty over ancestral lands which are in territories currently considered to be under the jurisdiction of a U.N. member state. On a more philosophical level, although even here there are political implications, demands of indigenous peoples for the recognition of their cultural rights challenge some of the most fundamental assumptions associated with human rights. In particular, the notion that individuals are ultimately the bearers of rights as "trumps," limiting the authority of governments to coerce behavior, appears to be at odds with indigenous peoples' claims to group rights.[1] From many indigenous points of view, there are no individuals who are not constitutively formed by and identified with groups and who do not owe significant loyalty to group traditions. Further, from such perspectives, liberal political assumptions of human rights have been used as a way of breaking down indigenous forms of social organization, while building the power of modern sovereign states.[2] Thus, again from these perspectives, the notion of individual human rights supports intrusion into indigenous affairs, acquisition of what are regarded as ancestral and religious lands, and correlative restrictions on the freedom of indigenous peoples to practice their religious traditions.

As a practical matter, the notion of collective or group rights may be able to co-exist with the notion of individual rights, at least in certain situations. According to Charles Taylor, for example, it may be possible to argue that in respecting the collective rights of Francophones in Quebec, the Canadian government is also respecting the rights of many individuals in Quebec who see the preservation of French language and culture as important to their personal identities.[3] And, speaking philosophically, there may be no necessary opposition between notions of group rights and emphasis placed on individual rights. Nevertheless, significant issues are implied in the juxtaposition of these two emphases. The Native American historian John Mohawk, for example, appears

---

[1] The notion of rights as "trumps" is borrowed from Ronald Dworkin, *Taking Rights Seriously* (Cambridge: Harvard University Press, 1977).

[2] Such a state, by its very nature, tries to create a homogenous society and culture within a given territory, whether this be in terms of the nation-state (where the language and culture of a particular group is recognized as dominant) or in terms of the pluralistic state (where the requirments of commonality are restricted to loyalty to institutions of government and to practices associated with a public morality). In either case, it appears that the advancement of the modern state involves a loss of sovereignty and power on the part of indigenous peoples.

[3] Charles Taylor, "The Politics of Recognition," in his *Multiculturalism and "The Politics of Recognition,"* with commentary by Amy Gutmann et al. (Princeton: Princeton University Press, 1992), pp. 25-73; see especially pp. 52-61.

to maintain that the practice of "tribalism" is a basic human need.[1] This position may challenge the social reality envisioned by human rights principles, which presuppose that the universal unity of human beings is more fundamental than the more particular unities of "tribalism." As indigenous peoples and their philosophies become more fully acknowledged in the regime of international human rights, we can expect it to be goaded and perhaps inspired by such challenges, possibly resulting in new human rights emphases and new directions of development.

CONCLUSION

In the end, the papers of this volume and participants in the Project's May meeting firmly agree that education and interreligious activity are appropriate and necessary to promote positive interactions between religion and human rights. There are some, of course, who may wish to criticize these proposed tasks as "typically liberal" approaches to problems of conflict and violence in human affairs—that is, as well-meaning approaches that nonetheless fail to address core causes of violence and mass human rights violations. Still others (to continue in this vein) may argue that the evils deplored by human rights advocates are finally ineradicable, as has been suggested in many of the most profound interpretations of the human condition. Nevertheless, no one would deny that we are obligated to seek at least proximate solutions to, or mitigations of, such evils. While we cannot do everything, we can at least do some things to address these problems, and we believe that the papers presented here provide evidence of the constructive role that religious traditions can play in mitigating the causes of violence and in fostering adherence to human rights norms. It is our collective responsibility to try to advance this constructive role, although we would be the first to concede that much work remains before us.

---

[1] John Mohawk in an interview with Kusumita P. Pedersen, transcript dated August 12, 1994. "Tribalism" is here understood in the sense of social practices by which personal identity and loyalties are formed and maintained in pervasive and enduring intimate relations.